GETTING A JUMP ON LIFE

Getting a Jump on Life

90 Years of Flying in the Face of Obstacles, Overcoming Hardships and Making My Own Way

AILEEN FRITSCH AND JACQUELINE MOSIO

Jacqueline Mosio

NORTH STAR PRESS OF ST. CLOUD, INC.
St. Cloud, Minnesota

ISBN: 0-87839-347-1
ISBN 13: 978-0-87839-347-3

Published in the United States of America by
North Star Press of St. Cloud, Inc.
PO Box 451
St. Cloud, MN 56302
www.northstarpress.com

Dedication

To all the people I love.
To all those who read my book, that they may be touched by the
Spirit of Adventure.

Aileen Fritsch

Table of Contents

Acknowledgements

From Aileen

Deep appreciation to all my family members for their love, support and the laughter we shared—and for providing me with the material for the stories I tell!

Special thanks to dear friends, wonderful neighbors, great helpers, and all those who came to the Gatherings on my porch.

From Jacqueline

Working with Aileen was a joy and privilege. Through her I came to know not only her family but her many fine friends.

Finishing the book gives me the opportunity to acknowledge the help and support I received.

The following people and institutions contributed to research: Brian Johnson at the Kennedy Krieger Institute of Baltimore; the Minnesota History Center Library; St. Paul Public Library and the five-star reference librarians; Duane Erickson of Lanesboro, Minnesota; and David Sandels, Capitol City Chapter of Antique Automobile Club.

Special thanks to editing assistants Christine Anderson and Kathryn-Ann Geis.

Much gratitude to my readers who offered comments and suggestions whenever I asked: Carole Nelson Douglas, Leo Erickson, Mary Firestone and Meryl Price.

To the Anderson Center for the Arts, Red Wing, Minnesota, for writing space. To Gail and Richard Keene for inviting me to stay and work at their magical San Miguel Allende home.

Great appreciation to Ron, Heidi, Mark, Joannie, Brian, and other members of Aileen's wonderful family for their cooperation, enthusiasm and patience.

Deep thanks to my family and friends for their unwavering interest and support.

৶ • ୡ

Introduction

Everyone who watched Aileen Fritsch leap out of that plane and drop through the sky on her ninetieth birthday felt that she broke barriers. With one step into thin air, she changed perceptions of what we can do, not only at age ninety but at any age and prompted people to think about how they want to live.

The petite, blond, energetic woman who did all that had a track record of doing things that got attention and changed expectations.

I inherited the skydiving, former nurse from my mother who met Aileen while attending nursing school. They remained close friends. Aileen was fascinating to me as a young girl. I watched this slim, self-confident, and lively woman sweep into our house. She joked, teased and told stories that made my parents laugh.

Her work was a cut different from that of the rest of my mother's nursing friends. As a private duty nurse, Aileen took care of wealthy people whose names I read in the newspaper. She worked odd hours and at night. She had an aura of mystery and adventure about her, and inevitably had some project up her sleeve or had just returned from an exciting trip. All this was intriguing to me. This was before the women's movement, before women claimed the right to be themselves. To me it seemed that Aileen was how women were supposed to be: aware, active, authentic, self-confident and intelligent.

Aileen moved with the precise and focused energy of a nurse and carried herself with a sense of competence and dedication. She was always thinking, ever engaged in the moment. Nothing got by her. A member of the "Greatest Generation," she worked through life's challenges on her own.

Aileen and I spent hours upon hours in interviews and discussions about her life and how to write her story. She wrote pages and read them to me. She responded to my promptings and questions. Her articulate and witty delivery provides the rich material in her book. As the writer, I shaped, rearranged and clarified material, expanded dialogue, and made connections. But this is her story in her words. And what words!

This is not merely the story of a feisty lady who lives life on her own terms. What emerges from these pages is the story of Aileen's journey into adulthood and her soul's growth through the heavy responsibilities and daunting challenges of her life.

Aileen's jump is a powerful metaphor that describes what she did every day: step through the door of the new day with trust, dance on the way down, and land with exhilaration even if things don't always work out perfectly.

Jacqueline B. Mosio
St. Paul, Minnesota
September 6, 2009

GETTING A JUMP ON LIFE

ॐ 1 ☙

Jumping into It

I'm doing it! I am in this plane and I'm really going to jump. I had better jump. The *St. Paul Pioneer Press* did a story on me, and a camera crew from WCCO TV, the local CBS affiliate, is down there waiting for me. I seemed to have caused quite a stir. I don't know why. I've watched a lot of programs about skydiving and always thought it looked like fun. Definitely something I'd want to do. So here I am.

I'm sure people wonder why I would want to go skydiving for my ninetieth birthday. Probably when you finish reading my life story, you'll say, "No wonder she wants to jump out of an airplane!"

I've always felt life is an opportunity that has to be taken advantage of before it slips away. What's the term people use today—proactive? As a kid, when life got too quiet and ordinary, I always thought of something to shake things up. I don't know how much my attitude and efforts were appreciated by others around me, but life wasn't dull for long if I had anything to do about it.

Jumping from a plane is certainly a way to inject some energy into this stage of my life. Growing old isn't a lot of fun in itself, is it? Why not see what will make it better and more interesting, what will bring

1

new people into my life, and show others what can be done. In other words, get a jump on this business of life. When I saw ninety coming over the hill, I figured I needed to do something fun and interesting. And that's what I'm doing. Under the jump suit, I'm wearing pink, my favorite color. I even dyed my tennis shoes pink!

The plane is circling around dropping other parachutists. I see all different looks on their faces as they head for the door. Most are eager and excited. A few look nervous. Today's not the greatest day to be jumping. The weather is overcast and drizzly. But we're doing it anyway. It's almost my turn.

I'm securely attached to Kerry McCauley, my handsome, delightful and confidence-inspiring jumping partner. He's going to guide me through this crazy jump. He's also the owner of Skydive Twin Cities, based at the Baldwin, Wisconsin, airport where we're doing the jump.

When we met, I said, "Kerry, I usually don't mention my age or have regrets about being the age I am. But this is one time I wish I were sixty years younger."

"I'm already spoken for," he responded with a warm twinkle in his eye.

Kerry has briefed me on what to expect and what happens when we jump out of the plane. I'm fascinated and eager to go. I've been wrapped, packed, zipped up, buckled in and attached. I'm getting antsy. I want to see what happens.

The plane is emptying out. Now it's our turn. We take our positions at the door. This is good. I was getting claustrophobic inside the plane. I know I'll prefer the wide-open space out there.

Wind whooshes at the plane's door as our photographer positions himself outside and hangs on, waiting for us to jump. Kerry counts one, two, three and out we go.

Falling, falling, buffeted by the wind. Flying—almost like a bird! Freedom. That's the sensation. I love it!

The cameraman maneuvers around us. Kerry taps me on the shoulder to give the thumbs up sign. What an experience! We're dropping through the sky. Hmmm. Feels like instant face lift.

Kerry gives me the signal that the parachute will open and then our free fall ends abruptly. Now we dangle and float. I swing my legs and dance in the air. I can twirl around. This is unbelievable! What fun! Why didn't I do this sooner!

I can see so far. The landscape is dotted with tidy farms like the one I grew up on in North Dakota. Houses and buildings nestle together. Toy cars zip along the roads. So this is how a bird feels. No wonder they sing and seem so happy. I always envied them soaring through the sky. I'd love to meet a few as I drift down. Can you believe it!

Friends asked me if I told my children about this jump. Not until I had made the reservation and paid the money. How do you tell your kids you're going to jump out of a plane? I certainly wasn't going to ask permission.

People say I'm not realistic about my age. I think I'm quite realistic. My vanity license plates say RETREAD.

The airport's down there with all my friends watching me. They are probably going to have sore necks from craning their heads up to see me.

I spot Ron on his red scooter. There are my other two kids, Mark and Heidi. Mark always asks me why I do the things I do. "I don't have any idea," I tell him. The grandchildren are watching me. It'll be fun for them to tell their classmates that they watched their grandmother skydive. Along with baking chocolate chip cookies for my grandkids, I decided to do something they'd really remember.

The thought occurs to me: Why would anyone want to read about my life? So many people are writing books these days. But I decided to persist with an idea I've had for a long time and get my story out there. I believe that there has to be something worthwhile between the covers of a book, something that makes the time you spend with a book meaningful. I'm going to have faith that there will be that meaning in my story just as I had to have faith at each turn of events in my life. Just as I have faith that I'll land okay and this jump will turn out fine.

My landing is going to be perfect. That's what I told everybody. I promised to do a better job than the senior Bush. No landing on my bottom for me! Once I land, we'll go to my church for a birthday party with all my family and friends.

Who would have thought that a rascally farm kid from Towner, North Dakota, would be skydiving into the next phase of her life!

What a jump!

What a life!

℘ 2 ℘

Canaries on the Prairie

I was born on June 27, 1914, between one and two in the afternoon. That afternoon, the Ladies' Aid Society was meeting at church, and my mother was supposed to serve. My grandmother was quite upset that I had to be born exactly at that time. "Maybe you could come for a little while and help," her mother-in-law suggested to my poor mother who was already feeling contractions.

The local midwife, Mrs. Shipman, delivered me and all the children in the area. I was my mother's first and was named Aileen Helen after my Swedish grandmother who raised birds and wanted my mom to help out at church the day I was born. Grandmother Ekstrom was from Stockholm, Sweden. Her mother (my great-grandmother) was a lady-in-waiting to the queen of Sweden, and my grandmother was born near the royal castle in Stockholm. At least that's the story as I heard it.

Grandmother Ekstrom loved her birds. She had learned how to raise canaries in Stockholm and brought the skill to America with her. For as long as I can remember, she tended her Jubilee Warblers, as she called them, in a room built onto a corner of her kitchen. It had special isinglass windows and a thermometer. The room had to be kept warm no matter what the temperature was outside on the North Dakota prairie.

I loved going over to her house to see the birds. When they were laying their eggs, we had to whisper. After they hatched she'd tell us, "Shhhh! Don't make any noise. We can't disturb them."

The birds lived in beautifully ornate wooden cages. She sold her canaries to customers in New York. Her warblers were guaranteed to sing, and she made a lot of money from them. Letters to her came addressed "Dear Bird Lady." She was very skillful and worked with the birds to make sure they sang. She hummed and sang when she was in their room to accustom the birds to singing. If one of them didn't sing loudly enough, she'd stand right next to the bird and talk to it. It was as if she were teaching in a school for birds. When they were ready, she would ship the birds to her customers by rail. From what I was told, the railroad men cared for the birds all along the way. They regarded it as a special privilege to watch out for her birds and make sure they were all right. She never had a single one returned because it didn't sing.

My grandmother fascinated me. I remember she was always well-groomed and she dressed with an elegance not usually seen in small towns. She wore beautiful dresses and blouses with frothy jabots at the neck. Her hair was braided and held in place with hairpins that glittered. She wore her braid like a crown. To me she looked like a queen.

Grandmother kept a big hatbox near her huge carriage bed that was covered with a cloud-sized feather comforter. I would jump on the bed when I slept over. The hatbox held gorgeous hats that a cousin of hers in New York sent her. Once she got a hat with a stuffed white bird on it. Grandmother was furious that a bird had been killed for a hat. She never wore that hat.

Her husband, my grandfather Pehr Ekstrom, was also born and raised in Stockholm. He had sailed around the world twice as a ship's captain. Everyone addressed him as Captain Ekstrom. The name, shortened from Ekstrommer when my grandfather came through immigration, means "strong oak." I don't know why my grandparents decided to homestead in North Dakota—perhaps because of other Swedish immigrants in the area. Along with their farm, my grandfather ran a dray line with horses. I remember him as tall and very distinguished-looking with his white silvery hair and beard. On my father's side of the family, all the men were at least six feet tall and the women were tall as well. Captain Ekstrom never left the house without his silk hat and the gold-headed cane that had been presented to him in Sweden. When he walked along the street, he tipped his hat to every lady he met.

Grandfather Ekstrom loved to read. He was a follower of Darwin's thought and described himself as an evolutionist. His room was filled with books and nautical instruments. He taught us grandkids the names of stars and how to use a sextant to locate position by the stars.

Unfortunately, Grandfather had poor eyesight. He was hit by a train—he didn't see it. They brought him home with a severe concussion and put him to bed. The doctor said he wouldn't last long. We all gathered around glumly waiting for his death. I was about eight years old, and it was unimaginable to me that anything could happen to Grandfather. He was such an important part of our lives. We were all feeling sad and resigned as we sat together in the kitchen. Suddenly, he burst through the door wrapped in a blanket with a lampshade on his head and another blanket over his arm. "Ladies," he announced, "I think I'm going to leave now." His mind was a little off, but he was up and walking and he did recover fully.

Grandfather Ekstrom had given my grandmother yellow diamond earrings for their wedding that he had brought back from a seafaring trip. She always wore the canary diamonds. They sparkled like the sun when she moved her head. When she died, he insisted that the earrings be left on her. We asked him why. "They belong to her," he said, "and I'll be able to find her when I get to heaven because she'll be wearing them."

After my grandmother died, their daughter, my Aunt Anna, who was widowed by then, came with her family to live with my grandfather. He was over ninety. For his ninetieth birthday, the businessmen and bigwigs of our town gave him a gold watch. In winter, no matter how cold it was, he would stand outside chopping wood everyday. I think my grandfather died just the way he planned. It was in the fall of the year, and he had been out chopping wood. He was carrying a whole armload of wood and sat down on the bench by the back door. When Aunt Anna called him to eat, she discovered that he had died. I never found out who inherited my grandfather's gold-headed cane or his gold watch.

My mother's parents, being from Norway, were quite different. Their families were farmers and fishermen from Bergen near the fjords and the Telemarken region. My mother, Nettie Haugen, came to America as an infant with her parents and two brothers. We still have a large painted tongue-and-groove wooden chest with my grandfather's name and identification number on it—Jorgen Haugen. They settled in Fosston in northern Minnesota near Crookston where other family members were already farming. We visited them often. We used the Norwegian *Bestefar* for Grandfather and *Bestemor* for Grandmother. My grandfather learned English quite well, but Bestemor refused to speak English. She hadn't wanted to come to America and this was her silent revolt. Unless we spoke Norwegian around her, she wouldn't talk to us. The community was a close-knit group and Norwegian was their main language. Everyone went to the Norwegian Lutheran church, the only church in town. Kids learned English at school but spoke Norwegian at home. Even the dogs barked in Norwegian.

My grandparents lived in Fosston until I was about ten or twelve years old. Then my mother brought her parents down to our farm. We had built a larger house across the yard from the house I had been born in. My grandparents lived in that house. In the evenings, my grandmother made *rømmegraut* for us—a thick porridge of flour and heavy cream. She also made *rosetter* using a special metal utensil that looks like a large flower-shaped cookie cutter on a stick. I loved watching her dip it into the creamy batter then plunge the coated flower into hot oil that churned and bubbled ominously. Then, when it was done, the delicate

8

golden brown, flower-shaped pastry serenely floated to the surface. After draining them, Bestemor sprinkled them with sugar and cinnamon. Even if they were for later, she would let me have one right then. The sweet spice taste exploded in my mouth as I bit into the crisp pastry. I made sure to thank her in Norwegian.

Bestemor was a petite, energetic, spicy person. On that side of the family they are small. Physically, that's the side I take after.

When my grandfather died at age eighty-eight, Bestemor moved across the yard into our house. She'd sit in the low rocking chair that they had brought with them from Norway. The chair was painted with traditional Norwegian designs called rose mauling. Bestemor liked our Lutheran minister because he was from Norway too. He often came out to visit and speak Norwegian with her. He was the pastor in town for fifty-one years. Summer and winter, he wore a wool suit, tie and shirt with cufflinks. He was always formally dressed. My mother spoke Norwegian but not as fluently as the pastor. Bestemor died ten years after her husband at age ninety-eight.

My parents met at Devil's Lake—a big resort lake that back then even had cruise boats. My mother worked as a waitress in a restaurant there with two friends. My dad met my mom when he visited the resort with some buddies. He always told us she was "quite a cutie." They were married in Fosston. My Norwegian mother and her Swedish husband, John William Ekstrom, immediately settled on a farm near his parents' place outside of Towner, North Dakota, near Minot and close to the Canadian border. Besides running our farm, my father operated the local grain elevator and served as fire chief of the volunteer fire department for forty-five years.

My mother was in her late thirties when I was born. She had four children in all, but Edna Karin, born two years after me, died from pneumonia at age two. My sister, Ruth Mamie, was four years younger and my brother, John Verner, was nine years younger. The death of my little sister affected my mother deeply, and little Edna was a bond between us. When Ruth was born just nine months after my mother lost Edna, it was very hard for her. She just wasn't there for Ruth, so essentially my father took over. Ruth was daddy's girl, and he treated her like a princess. Ruth was quite intelligent, and she did very well in school receiving many awards and playing in recitals—in general, an ideal daughter. I, on the other hand, seemed to have established my notorious character by age four. When Karin died, my Aunt Anna told my parents, "Don't worry about Aileen dying. Nothing's going to happen to her. Neither the devil nor the Lord wants her."

Our life on the farm was planned around the cows. We had to get up early to feed them. We had to get back home in time to milk them and we had to stay around for calving season in the spring. Like all farmers in the early decades of last century, we were self-sufficient. Sugar, flour and raisins were about the only food we bought. Everything else we raised and processed ourselves. We canned everything from the pig except its squeal. The pig's bladder got washed, blown up and used as a football—the original pigskin. All farm kids grew up playing with pigskin footballs.

In the cellar, we had carrots stored in barrels of sand, ropes of sausage hanging from the rafters, and jars of canned sauerkraut and canned meat lining the shelves. We had a smokehouse, so there was a lot of smoked and dried meat as well. Mother always baked her own bread. I never saw a loaf of store-bought bread in the house. In town there were freezers to rent for storing meat. Before those freezers were available, Mother had to can all the meat. Even with ice in the cellar, it wasn't cold enough to safely freeze meat.

Mother made underwear for the babies out of men's old long johns. Home medicine was an art and a science practiced by farm women. Mother had a book about household medicine, but she went beyond it. Neighbors came to consult with her. She was always whipping up drinks, making mustard plasters or administering some cathartic treat-

10

ment for illness. I remember that vanilla extract—expensive and hard to get—was the most precious item in the house. She was furious when she discovered that her sister-in-law's husband drank up one of the two bottles she had purchased to have on hand.

Mother wasn't the only one with special homemade remedies. A mile from us lived Bill Pitts who was part Indian. He hunted skunks and sold skunk oil lotion as a treatment for colds. Every time I had a cold, I had skunk oil rubbed on my chest. It wasn't bad smelling, but the idea of skunk oil gave me a fit.

My family had large gardens, and I had my tasks in the garden. I spent most of my time outside anyway so that was fine with me. I was not an indoor person. Starting at age seven, I worked summers combining in the fields. The combine was pulled by a team of horses. My job was to drive the horses forward and keep them moving straight. When the team moved forward, that lifted up the forks and pulled in the hay. There were thick ropes all around where I was sitting. I was so close to the action that I got a scar on my hip from rope burn. I told my dad, "Hey, look! I'm branded just like the cattle."

I loved haying season and working in the fields. I wore coveralls all the time. I never wanted to be a girl. To me it was pitiful that every Saturday I had to wash my hair and wrap it in rags to curl it so I'd look nice for church on Sunday.

I did get confirmed as an Episcopalian in my father's church. But it was a small congregation—only two other families, so the Episcopalian church closed after my confirmation. Then we went to the Lutheran church. That made my mother happy.

One time the Lutheran minister came to call. Now my mother—and probably the other Lutherans in town—opposed all liquor. Yet she used to make chokecherry wine to use on special occasions but didn't want anyone to know about it. On this occasion, however, she had corked the wine too soon. All through the minister's visit we could hear the explosions of the corks popping off the wine bottles in the kitchen.

We had a shared phone line and I would listen in on conversations. Everyone on the phone line had their own special ring so I knew who was getting a call. When things got a little dull or when we had to stay in for long stretches during winter, I listened in on some interesting calls. I lifted the receiver very carefully so as not to make any noise. I found out a lot about people and life through that phone line.

North Dakota winters, especially up near the Canadian border, are famous for blizzards, howling winds, and huge snowfalls. We took hard winters in stride. It was normal to have snow several feet high covering everything in sight. Although we didn't live too far from town, there'd be days when no one left the house except to go to the barn and tend the animals. We had thick ropes strung from the house to the barns. To go out, especially in a storm, I had to hold on tight to the rope and follow it carefully if I didn't want to end up frozen in a snow bank. At times snow fell so thickly I couldn't see a foot ahead of me. With all our stored food we survived without having to go to town. Even in the worst of winters, when we couldn't get out for days, we never ran out of food.

Winter was made more bearable because of Christmas and the many holiday rituals. All the farms had sleighs and horses. On Christmas Eve my dad brought out a large flatbed and covered it with hay. He hitched up the horses Molly and Sue and put bells on their harnesses. A dozen or so people—friends and family—settled onto the straw, and we drove into town a mile away to go caroling at friends' houses. After that we came back to our house where our *lefse* and *lutefisk* dinner was waiting for us.

Lutefisk is the Scandinavian delicacy that folks in Minnesota joke about. It's cod preserved in lye and imported from Norway. The *lutefisk* came in huge slabs, solid as a rock. It had to be soaked for three days before Christmas and then boiled. Now it comes in tidy plastic packages. However, it still retains its characteristic, unmistakable fishy fragrance.

Lefse is a tortilla-like bread made from potatoes. Making *lefse* was quite a project that would take place a few days before Christmas. When I left home and couldn't get back for Christmas, Mother would often send me a package of her homemade *lefse*. She also made *sunbakkle*, a delicious little pastry filled with dates and nuts that was a special treat.

We would be very quiet as Grandfather Ekstrom made a beautiful Christmas speech. Then we'd go into the living room and gather around the tree. It had real wax candles in metal holders that clipped to the tree branches. Gifts were distributed and opened. One Christmas my Aunt Anna, who always joked with me, gave me the game called Old Maid because she figured no one would ever want to marry me. After the gifts, the candles on the tree were blown out and the children went to bed to wait and see what Santa Claus would bring on Christmas morning.

Every Christmas my mother told this story from her childhood. She was six years old and had never owned a doll. That Christmas, the Lutheran Church was going to give out dolls and toys to the children. Her parents bundled her up and drove the horse and buggy all the way into town from their farm. My mother was so excited. She could see her new doll and feel it in her arms. She had made a special place for the doll to sleep in her bed. But when they arrived, there were no more dolls left. All the way back home to the farm my mother felt so sad. On Christmas morning, though, she opened her eyes and saw a doll sitting at the foot of her bed. It was so beautiful and finely dressed that she could hardly believe the doll was real. She held it in her arms—her first doll. Her father had stayed up all night carving the doll out of wood while her mother sewed the doll's dress using her own clothes and had cut her own hair to use for the doll's hair.

ॐ 3 ॰

My Childhood Reputation

I was born into a wonderful family that had interesting people. I grew up in a wide-open space where I could roam, explore and feel free. I needed that. I like open spaces. I think my parents were happy I had so much space to run around and wander in. I also had horses to race and animals to care for. I love doing things and there's always something to do on a farm. But I also love being with people and find others fascinating. Of course, I had strong opinions about people and clearly wasn't timid about acting on them.

I wonder if in today's terms my behavior would be called acting out. Or maybe I would have been diagnosed with attention deficit disorder. I had a reputation that I worked hard for. We attended a small Episcopalian church in town. On a particularly cold and snowy Sunday when the pastor had left his galoshes outside, I got my friend Marjorie to help me fill them with water.

Living on a farm with many relatives around gave me opportunities to cultivate my curiosity and learn everything I could. Aunt Anna, my dad's sister, taught me to read and write before I went to school. She loved to read and would wash dishes with a book propped up at the sink. She gave me books. My dad tended all the animals himself and had lots of veterinary books. I read them and learned about the birds and bees that way. I really wanted to be a surgeon and to operate. I used to cut open whatever I could get my hands on. I'd catch snakes and beetles then take them apart—all kinds of things. I wanted to know what made them tick.

Mother used a wire brush to comb my long hair, braiding it so tight that whatever expression I started out with in the morning I kept all day. She put two braids on top and two below and fastened them together. For me, braids were better than when she put rags in my hair to give me curls. It was hard trying to sleep on the lumpy rags. Then she'd put a big bow on my head just for Sunday. Maybe that was why I filled the pastor's boots with water. I put up with the braids. I wanted to chop off my hair like the boys, but my dad said he'd keep me in the basement until it grew back. I believed him so I didn't cut it. But I hated having my hair fussed over.

My sixth birthday was coming. Mother told me, "You're going to have a birthday party just like the other girls with ice cream and angel food cake and pretty clothes and nice, curly hair." Later, when I had moved away, she always made me an angel food cake with thirteen egg whites for my birthday and sent it to me no matter where I was.

But I was very definite about not having a party. I told her that I didn't want a party with the girls, I didn't want ribbons in my hair or my hair tied up with rags the night before. I didn't want to get dressed up. No matter, she said, I was going to have a party. I wasn't at all happy with that, so I went and gathered lots of garter snakes and put them in a bucket in the garden. And I found an ax. The girls arrived all dressed up and pretty. They brought me presents. I told them to come and see something real unusual. They watched as I kicked over the bucket and chopped up the snakes that came wriggling out. The girls ran away screaming and went home. My mother was so upset. This was clearly not a nice thing to do. She gave back the presents, but I didn't want them anyway. In my opinion, they were just silly, girly things.

I had no time for dolls. I never liked them and never played with dolls except for one—Sarah, a rag doll, the only doll I liked. After my dad bought me boxing gloves, I didn't play with girls anymore. Instead I played with the boys. They'd punch me but I never complained even though I got a couple of black eyes. My father figured he should teach me how to box to take care of myself. He'd invite the boys over and put the boxing gloves on my hands and I'd pound away at them. No boys picked on me, I can assure you. But that didn't keep me from picking on others—even my teachers.

Mr. Coe was my third grade teacher. I must have decided it was my mission to make his life miserable. I invented a song that I taught the other students: "Mr. Coe stubbed his big toe. All the kids went ho, ho, ho!"

He always helped out a girl who sat near me. She was very pretty and had lots of bouncy naturally curly hair while I wore my long straight hair in braids on either side of my head like curved ram's horns. When he bent over her desk, his pants bagged out. I didn't like baggy pants. I had spotted a huge red ant hill on our church property. One day I collected some red ants in a jar and brought them to school. That day when Mr. Coe bent over the curly-haired girl's desk, I poured the ants into his pants pocket. Then I got up, went for my coat and walked home. My mother saw me coming up the road. She came to the door and said, "Aileen, Aileen. What have you done now?"

Of course I was suspended from school for several days for that one. My delight in my prank was sharply diminished by the fact that all those days at home my mother put me to work. We had a hardwood floor in the kitchen and she made me scrub it with lye. That took up almost the whole time I was out of school.

Once when I was eight and had done something particularly bad, I ran away from home. I packed food, a blanket, and a pillow. My plan was to hide in the cornfield all night. A few hours went by out there. I heard my parents calling me. Finally I decided to go visit a neighbor, Mr.

Miller, who lived near the river. I went to his house. He gave me milk and cookies and called my parents.

It was my job to care for my baby brother who was nine years younger. His problem—other than having me as his sister—was that he cried a lot. He had eczema, which made him a very fussy baby, and I got tired of taking care of him. One day when I was pushing him in his buggy trying to distract him, I saw a group of Gypsies. They came every summer and camped a quarter of a mile from the farm on the riverbank. I had heard that they would take children, so I decided to give my yelling, squalling brother to the Gypsies. I was heading across the field, pushing the buggy over the furrows, but before I reached them, my dad spotted me and asked where I was going with Johnny. "I'm going to give him to the Gypsies because all he does is scream," I told him. My father was furious with me. I got my usual castor oil treatment.

I don't remember ever being hit or spanked by either parent. But when I intentionally did things I shouldn't have, I'd get castor oil as a punishment—one tablespoonful if I didn't resist, two if I did. So I just opened my mouth and swallowed it. Later I thanked my folks. I told them that due to the castor oil I never had constipation problems my whole life.

I always wondered about the connection between castor oil, misbehavior and intestines. Perhaps the idea was to flush out the bad behavior. Or maybe it was a way to control me for a while. I couldn't get into any more mischief at least until I had gone to the bathroom and spent a while on the throne, as we called it.

My father had purchased a new bull. The vet came out to put a copper ring in the bull's nose, but they couldn't find the copper ring my dad had bought. Of course they couldn't find it. I was wearing it. I saw it and slipped in on my arm that morning when I went off to school. I didn't have much jewelry, and I thought it was pretty. It was my first bracelet.

The vet had to drive all the way back the next day. My father said, "I wonder if they have a ring that will fit your nose. Then at least, when I tie you up to a post, I'll know what you're doing."

We grew a lot of potatoes in the garden. My parents assigned me the job of picking bugs off the potato plants. We didn't use pesticides back then, so the bugs had to be gotten rid of by hand. I had to hit the plants with a long fork to make the bugs fall into a large pan. This involved scrabbling through the potato vines and dealing with the creepy bugs that often ended up on my arms and legs. The task was disgusting, and I thought it was unfair that I had to do it. As I watched the bugs plunk into the pan and crawl around, I came up with a plan. First, I short-sheeted my parents' bed and then dumped the pan of potato bugs into it. They were so mad. That time I got two tablespoons of castor oil poured into me.

It wasn't that I was a bad kid. It's just that life would get too quiet. I could always figure out something to do to liven things up like putting frogs in Miss Munkabe's desk. She was the teacher in charge of morning assembly and had a fixed routine. Every morning she opened her top desk drawer, pulled out her white hankie, shook it, and delicately patted her mouth. After that ritual she would speak to the assembly. One morning she opened the drawer and out jumped a dozen froggies.

I never lacked things to do to create mischief, but I didn't act out of meanness. I think I was just observant and inventive. My pranks and adventures took planning. With the ants for Mr. Coe's pants, for example, I had to figure out how to catch enough of them. It took me two days. First, I tried to pick them up with a spoon. That didn't work. They moved too fast. Besides, I had to keep watch to make sure no one saw me. I finally used sugar to get the ants I needed.

My dad had purchased a nice new car. I carefully watched to see how he drove and shifted the car. Everyday he came home from work for lunch then took a nap on the couch. The car was just sitting there, so I decided to take the kids for a ride in it. I put my brother and sister in the front seat and started the car. I drove it around the farm, then pulled up in front of the house and honked.

Dad came flying out and started chasing me. I jumped out of the car and ran across the field to my grandmother's house. Grandma Ekstrom saw me coming. "What did you do now?" she asked as I ran in the back door. "Quick. Go hide under the bed."

Dad drove up in the car and looked around the house. He couldn't find me. My grandmother didn't say anything. But I lost on that one because the circus was in town, and as my punishment I wasn't allowed to go.

When I was about seven or eight, my dad bought a horse for me. It was a pinto. We called them Indian ponies, and I took care of him. I had a saddle, but I liked riding bareback. I was a farm girl, and I rode my pony all over, even to town. It was a great way to go to town. My pony's name was Choppy—he had a terrible gait, but he was a good jumper. I'd put down whipple trees to build a barrier. We'd ride toward it. Then I'd poke him in the ribs with my heels and he'd run and jump over the barrier. I had Choppy for about six years until we sold him when I was twelve or thirteen. The horse I got next wasn't a purebred. He was different shades of tan like a Palomino.

I enjoyed dressing in cowboy clothes with the hat and the works—chaps, boots, vest, jacket. My dad would get me whatever I wanted to wear. Not many of my friends had horses nor did my sister Ruth, who didn't like horses. As far as I was concerned, she didn't do anything. She was "a lady." I wasn't.

My father's favorite summation of me was that I was the poorest possible advertisement for a dairy farm in the world—skinny with never an ounce of fat on me. Not only was I skinny, I wore coveralls all the time. I wouldn't wear shoes to school, only boots—lace-up work boots. I never dressed up except on Sundays and that was because my mother said the Lord would be looking straight at me. No one who knows my enjoyment of fashionable clothes throughout my adult life would ever believe I was such a tomboy. I remember once when I did dress up, my dad said, "Oh, that's nice. You can look like a young lady."

Life on our North Dakota farm was busy for me and full of memories. I wasn't always up to major mischief, I'm happy to recall. In our yard we had a giant cottonwood tree. I asked my father if I could build a tree house way up in the branches. "Yes," he said. "That would be a nice place for one. I'll help you build it." It was wonderful working with my father. First he drove spikes into the tree trunk where the house would be. Then he nailed wooden boards into place for the floor. Next came the boards for three sides, then the roof was nailed on. To me it was so beautiful.

Mother gave me a rag rug for the floor and two pretty red pillows for my tree house. I would bring my kitten up there, but she had to be petted all the time or she wouldn't stay with me. I liked dogs better. Maybe that's why the kitten wouldn't stay with me. My mom liked cats, though.

When the squirrels played on the roof, they made a lot of noise. I fixed up a small bucket of grain for the birds and hung it on a nearby branch.

I wanted to sleep overnight in the tree house, and I tried to figure out how to get Mother to let me. It would have been fun, but she always said no. However, she did bring me cookies and milk.

On hot days, my tree house was nice and cool. The leaves of the tree rustled all around me. When it rained, it was fun to hear the raindrops patter on the roof while I was snug and dry inside.

I had my books up there with me and especially liked stories about animals. I also drew stick people on my big tablet—round heads and straight lines for the body, legs and arms—and made up stories about them. What a happy time I had in my very special tree house. I'm sure my parents were relieved. For once they knew where I was and they figured I wasn't going to get into any trouble.

All farm kids got their driving licenses young. I was ten when I got mine for ten cents so I could drive the milk truck into town. Whenever I drove the truck, we had to put blocks of wood on the pedals so I could reach them.

In the summertime, we had to move the cattle to another grazing ground. When I herded cattle, I had all sorts of time to myself. I could dream, think about my future, watch the bugs in the grass and read. The magazine we got on the farm was *The Farmers' Digest*—which used to be *The Country Gentleman*. I read every page of that and whatever other magazines people gave me. I also borrowed books from our tiny public library. I read lots of books.

I loved herding the cows. I'd move them and they'd graze awhile. My horse would lie down. There weren't any fences, so I had to keep all the cows in view. Because it was open land, sometimes a cow would run off as I was moving them, and I had to chase after her to round her up. I had to move them every day and bring them back in the evening to the corral a half a mile from the house. Old Shep, our farm dog, guided the cows into the corral and helped my dad, mother, and the hired hand get the cows into their stalls for milking. Our dairy cows were milked by hand. We took them out to graze every day except when it was raining. It was a good job, and I liked it. But I didn't like milking the cows.

Father thought it would be a good idea for me to learn to milk so I could help out on weekends when I didn't have to go to school. He showed me how. "Oh, this is easy," I told him. But every time I milked the cows, they would kick and pull away from me and get agitated. He would have to come around and calm them down. My poor father was quite frustrated. Finally he said, "Aileen, go back to the house and don't ever come around the barn at milking time again. I just don't know how somebody so smart in school can be too dumb to milk a cow."

I was determined not to get stuck with cow milking, and I suc- ceeded. I pinched their teats really hard instead of smoothly pulling the milk out, so of course the cows protested.

At about age twelve, I started getting serious with myself. My confirmation was approaching and I wanted to prepare myself. I wondered why I was always in trouble and pulling pranks that upset people so much. I was a member of the church choir and knew where the communion wafers were kept. I decided to eat them all. I had thought about this for a long time. If I ate a lot of them, I reasoned, maybe I'd get real holy and be cured of being so mischievous. I convinced Marjorie Weber to go along with me. We had choir practice Saturday night and that's when Marjorie and I snuck away to get the wafers from the cabinet where they were kept. We took out the box and opened it up. We started with a few and kept on going until we devoured all the wafers in the box. They were awfully dry.

"Do you feel holy yet?" Marjorie asked

"I don't know," I answered. "How is holy supposed to feel?" I didn't realize that the wafers had to be blessed first.

We put the empty box back.

At the service the next day, the deacon discovered there were no wafers for communion. He had to go across the street and get regular bread from Mrs. Elliot and cut it into cubes so we could have communion that morning.

It didn't take them long to figure out who did it. We told them we ate them up because we thought we'd get holy and be good.

I played with boys and had boys as friends, but I didn't date. We didn't have proms or special dances at school. We did go to barn dances, though, and I danced a lot. In my teens, I was friends with the deputy sheriff's daughter. He was the chaperone at the barn dances. By then I must had gotten interested in having curls. One Sunday I burned my tongue testing the curling iron while curling my hair. We were supposed to sing that day in front of everyone. I told my mom I couldn't go. My tongue was hanging out and I couldn't close my mouth. My mother said, "The Lord won't mind if your tongue is out as long as you're in church. Besides, you never close your mouth anyway, so it won't matter."

It was no wonder that when neighbors asked my mother if I could babysit their kids, she'd say, "No, not Aileen. But Ruth can." I think she was never too sure what I'd do with the little ones. Ruth, four years younger, was allowed to babysit. I remember that as I grew older, though, whenever there was a decision to be made around the farm, my parents always included me in the discussions. They treated me as an adult, trusted me and valued my opinion and experience in that sphere.

As I mentioned, my Aunt Anna taught me to read and write before I started school. She also taught me multiplication tables, addition, and subtraction before first grade. So when I was in the first grade, I studied some second grade material. In high school, I took advanced classes. By taking the accelerated courses, we could get through in three years instead of four. I graduated at age sixteen with a class that wasn't my original group. It wasn't that I was so bright. I was just able to work people and get them to go along with what I wanted!

I told myself, "I'm going to leave this place and see what else is out there." The wide world beyond my familiar open spaces was calling to me.

≈ 4 ≈

Nurses' Training and Bending Rules

B ecause I finished high school in three years, I was seventeen when I enrolled in pre-med at the University of Minnesota in Minneapolis. I lived at the dormitory and worked in the cafeteria for my food. I wanted to be a doctor and probably a surgeon.

During my freshman year, I almost married a guy who was studying to be a mortician. We met in a class. When we'd go out, he'd pick me up but then we'd stop by the morgue. I helped him with his cadavers. It was pretty gruesome. The bodies were in tanks of formaldehyde, but I couldn't see the people because their heads were wrapped. I was thankful for that. I didn't want to see them or have them stare at me!

After my first year, though, my parents could no longer afford to pay for my schooling at the university. The Depression had started. So I switched to nursing. I applied to the program at St. Luke's Hospital in St. Paul, Minnesota, and was accepted immediately. Nursing wasn't my first choice, but I enjoyed it.

In my little town of a bunch of farmers, if you didn't send your kids to college, you were on the low rung. Three-fourths of the young people went to teachers or agricultural college. My classmate Dorothy McDonald, another girl, and I all went into nurses' training.

24

My father said, "While you are there, remember that you have responsibilities." He was trying to tell me not to do anything too crazy. That was a hard order.

One hot early summer day I wanted to take a sunbath. I convinced Martha and Glenda to sunbathe in our bras and undies on the roof. We crawled through a duct and pushed open the trap door to get out onto the roof but forgot that the door shut and locked. We were trapped on the roof. So we oiled ourselves up and stretched out on our towels. No one could see us sunbathing. When we wanted to go back down, we had to lean over the edge of the roof and yell and holler to get the attention of people below. Someone finally saw us and reported that there were naked women screaming on the roof of the nurses' residence.

As part of our nursing program, we had classes in decorum and behavior. I'm not sure how much I benefited. At the residence, they checked our breath for alcohol and withheld passes if they suspected us of improper behavior. We had to be back in the dorm at midnight. That was pretty ridiculous. Parties and dances, especially on the weekends, didn't end before midnight. But our rooms were inspected to make sure we were there. When I knew I'd be out late on a Saturday date, I'd fix up my bed to look like I was asleep in it. My date would drop me off after a late party at Uncle Jay and Aunt Minnie's house. They were friends who had moved from North Dakota to St. Paul, but they were so close to our family that we called them aunt and uncle. Their house was conveniently near the nurses' residence. I was more than welcome at their place. In the morning, I'd walk over to a nearby church, blend with the crowd coming from services, and casually stroll back into the dorm and up to my room.

The nursing program at St. Luke's had a good reputation despite my efforts to buck the system. Nurses usually studied at training schools attached to hospitals like ours. That meant that we worked while studying. St. Luke's was affiliated with the University of Minnesota, so I continued taking classes at the university as part of our program. We rode back and forth on a green-colored bus that we nicknamed the "Protozoa"—a slow-moving, simple-celled life form.

As part of our training, we had to take water survival classes once a week at the YWCA pool eight blocks from the nurses' residence. We walked there and back. Our hair would freeze stiff in the winter. No hair blowers back then.

Our residence had a smoking room that was also our chatting room. If only walls could talk! So many things were said in that room. Some of my friends didn't approve of what went on there—the smoking and the gossip—and wouldn't join us.

One punishment for transgressing the rules was being sent to scrub down rooms after patients were released from the hospital. I got to do that on a regular basis. I had it down to a science and was pretty efficient. Julie, one of my nursing buddies who became a lifelong friend (she also grew up on a North Dakota farm), would stop me in the hall when she saw me coming out of a room carrying a bucket and mop. "Aileen, why do you do these things that you know will get you in trouble?" She thought I was terrible. "It's not only you," she continued. "You get others in trouble too." Julie wasn't as blatant and daring as I was. I never convinced her, but I always had an answer. "Look at it this way, Julie. I'm part of their education."

Another friend asked me after some particularly risky adventure, "What happens if you get thrown out of the nursing program?" I had met a guy named Joe at a Presbyterian church. He had a job at St. Paul Insurance Company. I thought to myself, if worse comes to worst, I'll just marry Joe and stay around here. Funny thing—the three guys I most cared about in my life were all named Joe. That certainly made it easy for me to remember them.

I was still in training when one of my classmates set me up on a blind date. He turned out to be very attentive and a good guy who always got me back to the dorm before curfew. After we had been going together a while, my mother came to visit, so his family invited us over for dinner. Before dessert was served, he stood up, made a little speech and presented me with a ring. I was shocked. For once I had no words. The next week his sister had a bridal shower for me and took me to see the apartment she had picked out for us. I broke off the engagement. That level of taking over my life wasn't what I wanted. In fact, no one was going to manage me. He eventually found someone else to marry, but the morning before his wedding he came to see me.

I also dated a local radio announcer for a while. He too gave me a ring, but I got mad at him one night and threw the ring out the car window. He stopped the car and told me to get out. It was dark, but my pride and anger wouldn't let me give in so I walked home.

Nursing in my day was quite different from now. We wore crisp white uniforms and caps, white hose, and shoes. It was clear who was a nurse on the floor. But we also did a lot of cleaning and hands-on patient care such as bathing and feeding patients that nurse aides and orderlies do today. I've seen so many changes in nursing and hospital practices! Health care always fascinated me whether I was reading about how to care for calving cows in my dad's veterinary books, watching my mother prepare a home remedy or running over to our neighbor Bill Pitts to get some of his skunk oil lotion. I worked in many medical settings and found the story of the hospital where I worked and trained typical of how a community cares for its sick and disadvantaged members. I can't help noticing the important role that women have played in health care over the years.

St. Luke's Hospital goes back to 1855 when a group of parishioners at Christ Episcopal Church decided to found a hospital and orphan's home in Minnesota. At that time, the village of St. Paul was a trading post at the head of navigation on the Mississippi River. Its five thousand white settlers were outnumbered by the Native American population. The Reverend John Van Ingen had arrived in 1854 from Rochester, New York. His daughter died soon after, and her death motivated him to establish a hospital and orphanage in 1857 under the name "Christ Church Hospital and Orphan's Home for Minnesota." The small wooden structure that had been donated soon proved inadequate so a minister's private home was used as the hospital. It served orphans and the sick who couldn't pay for their care.

Up until 1862, the hospital did this successfully, but then the medical staff left for the Civil War. Women from St. Paul's Episcopal Church maintained a home for invalids and children, giving free care until 1872. After reorganization, the hospital was revived and named Saint Luke's Hospital of Saint Paul. In 1891, a site at the corner of Smith and Sherman below the Summit Avenue bluff was purchased and a sixty-five-bed hospital was built.

The Saint Luke's School of Nursing opened in 1892, and a three-year nursing program was instituted in 1901. It became a general Protestant hospital in 1920 under the supervision of a number of Protestant churches. The Nurses Home was added in 1924. That's where I lived when I studied and worked at the hospital. The nursing school had an excellent reputation and required high school graduation for admittance rather than simply a grade school education. By the time it closed in 1936 due to the Depression, 593 nurses had graduated. I was one of them and graduated the year before it closed. My friend Julie was in the last graduating class. In 1972, St. Luke's joined with nearby Miller Hospital, located on lower Summit Avenue near the St. Paul Cathedral, where I also worked for a time, and became United Hospital with greatly expanded services.

During my three years of training, I'd regularly go home to North Dakota to visit my folks. When I arrived, my mother had me drag all the rugs outside, take down all the pictures, wash the woodwork and clean everything. I'd work the entire day. "At this rate," I told her, "you're not going to have a daughter for too long. You're going to kill me with so much work." Handing me a pail of soapy water, my mother said, "I've never seen a tombstone that reads 'Here lies someone who died of overwork.'"

I noticed that our nursing supervisors were all quite old. They seemed to live a long time. I wondered if long life had something to do with nursing!

When I graduated from St. Luke's three-year nursing program, I worked at the hospital for two months. I was paid sixty dollars a month plus room and board. Then I took off on the adventure that was to be my life. My first stop was the West Coast.

ഌ 5 ര

Go West, Young Woman

As a graduate of St. Luke's three-year nursing program, I could continue working at the hospital. Those of us who stayed just put on
our new white nurse caps the day we graduated and went back to work.
While still in St. Paul, I got a job offer for private duty nursing. This is
when a nurse is hired to take care of an individual, usually at home and
always for a wealthy person. I was hired by the James J. Hill family to
accompany a member of the family (James J. Hill was the Minnesota
railroad magnate who built the Great Northern Railway that spanned
the northern states west to Seattle) on a trip to his mansion in Pebble
Beach, California. It was my first year out of training, and I was happy
to have the job.

Margaret Ryan, another young nurse who had graduated from St.
Joseph's Hospital, and I went out west on the train with Mr. Hill in his
special railroad car. We then stayed with him at his mansion. Mr. Hill
had a trusted valet who took care of him. All we had to do was monitor
his blood pressure and give him his medications. We were not extremely busy, so we decided to see who could grow the longest fingernails.
Our contest went on to the point where we could hardly feed ourselves.

I don't recall who had the longest nails, but I do remember how hard it was to cut them off. We were out there for a few months then came back to St. Paul. So much for private duty nursing.

My West Coast experience whetted my appetite for travel. When Dorothy, another St. Joseph's Hospital graduate, told me she wanted to go out west, I arranged for us to stay at my aunt's house in Seattle, Washington. We found jobs quickly at a Seattle hospital. Good thing we did because within a week Dorothy had an appendicitis attack and needed surgery! Eventually Dorothy met a fellow named Karl and fell in love. They got married, and I lost track of her. I was on my own. I decided to change hospitals and went to Sisters of Providence hospital.

I liked working with the nuns. I always knew when the supervising nun, Sister Oliver, was coming because I could hear the clanking of her keys and the rosary beads that she wore as part of her religious habit.

For some reason whenever there were sick priests to take care of, the sisters sent in the non-Catholic nurses. When I'd leave the room of a priest I was attending, I'd always say, "Remember, Father, keep the faith!" Sister Oliver heard about it and said that I was irreverent.

I also worked in the IV department. Back then, intravenous solutions were made up at the hospitals through a filtration process. This was done using huge graduated glass vials with honeycomb filters. We had to pour sterilized water into gallon containers and filter it to make the IV solution. Sister Oliver told me each graduated vial cost several hundred dollars—a lot of money at that time.

"Sister, you should never have told me how much they cost. As sure as God is in heaven, I'll break one of them," I said.

"Just keep your mind on what you're doing," she instructed me. With her watching me, I never broke one. I would also go to patients' rooms to set up their IVs. I really liked this work. But sure enough, one day as I poured hot water into a vial, it cracked. Sister Oliver should never have told me how much it cost. For some reason, she didn't get mad at me. She was very kind to this Scandinavian Lutheran. I think I must have been one of the rare ones she met.

My cousin Helen in Seattle had beautiful horses, so soon I was out at the horse arena. I didn't have much money, but I rented a small mare called Nightingale. She was easy to ride and fun to jump. We rode English style, and I learned different gaits.

Then my dear little horse developed a kidney infection. Helen and I stayed up all night changing hot packs and taking care of her. We kept her standing with a harness and pulley because if she went down, she'd never get up again. She recovered, but my pocketbook took a deep hit. I paid the vet bill in very small installments. I had to decide if I would be able to afford riding. Nightingale was eating better than I was. I decided to ride less frequently. We were only paid once a month at the hospital. I had to get up considerable nerve to ask for an advance on my salary. They wanted to know why I needed the money. "For my horse," I told them. So they paid me in advance. I also began working six-day weeks. My pay was thirty dollars a week. Thank heavens I could eat my main meal at the hospital so I didn't starve to death. It was better food than at St. Luke's in St. Paul. There we had room and board but made only sixty dollars a month.

I never ate so much oatmeal in my life. A bag of raisins was gold to me. I never liked meat anyway so that wasn't a problem. All the time I had the horse, we were both eating oats! It's funny—I still like oatmeal mixed with a handful of raisins. It takes me right back to my Seattle days.

I was working nights at another hospital run by nuns. During the day I had been at the arena where I was exercising my horse for a show. I came back home and went to work at 10:30 P.M. We were up on the sixth floor psych ward in the preparation room. I was just telling another staff member about jumping my horse when I felt a jolt. It started then

32

stopped for a fraction of a second and continued—an earthquake. "Oh my God, the table is moving!" shouted the nurse I was talking to. All of a sudden, Sister Mary Anthony came striding down the hall splashing holy water all over. We were holding on to the walls and standing in doorways to protect ourselves. I called to Sister, "Don't waste the holy water on a Lutheran!" She got me all wet. She went through two flasks of holy water. I wasn't sure if the holy water worked for Lutherans. The earthquake was so bad that the cupola fell off the hospital building. Everything was shaking. Carts came flying down the hall. Patients were yelling and falling out of their beds then crawling into other beds. The quake was short, but the bedlam on the psych ward went on for hours.

I also worked at Swedish Hospital and later at Harbor View Hospital where we took care of people from the wharves. When they came in to the hospital, we dunked them in tanks of disinfectant to get the fleas off them. I spent some time in California as well and worked in a clinic near the San Francisco wharf. I shared an apartment with another nurse, and we kept live lobsters in the tub. When I wanted to take a bath, I had to transfer the lobsters to a pail, bathe, clean the tub real well, and then put the lobsters back into the tub.

My lifestyle was to work and save money. When I had enough, I'd take off, travel around and visit people until my money ran out. Then I'd get another job. It was easy to find work as a nurse.

I worked a while in Los Angeles at Cedars of Lebanon Hospital. We had to wear lipstick and a fresh hankie in our uniform pockets. Our uniforms fit like wallpaper. I worked there a few months and got some new uniforms. I didn't stay with them long enough to get integrated into the hospital. It was too much about show and that didn't appeal to me. I was also lonesome for Seattle so I went back there. I felt like a seagull going back and forth from Seattle to L.A. and beyond.

33

My brother John had moved to California and lived in San Diego. I took the bus to see him and we went to Tijuana together. I rode on the back of his motorcycle. We had a great time stopping at various bars, sampling tequila, eating lobster and shrimp and joining in hat dances. At one place there was a dance contest. I entered and won a beautiful vase. But I had to give it away. I couldn't take it with me on the back of the motorcycle.

One of my male friends was Fred Dupre, a professional mountain climber. He was really a dedicated climber. I always questioned my sanity with regard to Freddie. A date meant hanging by ropes from one mountain or the other. He was crazy about Mount Washington so we usually climbed it every weekend. I'd climb up to the first level with him, then pull out my book to wait for Fred to get back.

My next friend was a dog lover. Vincent had a beautiful greyhound that came with us on dates. The threesome was a bit overwhelming at times. Once when he had to go out of town, he asked if he could leave the dog with me. I said sure. He brought the dog over and left it. I went to bed. I had to get up early for work the next day. However, my bed was a Murphy bed that pulled out from the wall. The dog curled up to sleep under the bed. In the middle of the night, the dog stood up to stretch and turn around and pushed the bed back up into the wall. I was stuck upside down against the wall screaming. The bed can't be opened from the inside. Finally, my cousin Helen came home and rescued me. That was the end of my relationship with Vincent even though he bought me a beautiful cup and saucer as an apology for the mishap. I kept his gift but let him go.

After that I met Richard who was a horse lover like me. We rode together in the arenas and attended shows in the ring. One Christmas day we went on a paper hunt. Instead of hounds and a fox, someone goes ahead and leaves a trail of crumpled paper. The paper chase was a lot of fun. But Richard had to go back East to school at Harvard and our paths never crossed again.

Then came Joe Manning, a lieutenant in the Seattle vice squad. Joe was a burly Irishman with a keen sense of humor. Being with him was like having joined the circus. On dates we'd first stop at houses of ill repute in order to pick up the protection money the police department collected from the madams. These places were gorgeously decorated with luxurious furnishings. I was admitted only as far as the kitchen. I wanted to see more but no luck. Oh, well, so much for that phase of my education.

One night three couples rented a boat in Puget Sound. In the middle of the Sound, the motor died. We couldn't start it and began drifting. It was getting dark. The wind picked up and the waves kept getting bigger and more powerful. Finally the boat capsized, and we were tossed into the dark, turbulent water. Somehow we all managed to cluster around the boat and cling to it and each other. We hung on for what seemed like an eternity before a Coast Guard boat spotted us and rescued us. Guess it wasn't my time to die yet.

No grass grew under my feet. Between my boyfriends and my nursing jobs, I got quite an education during the years I lived on the West Coast. In fact, I did get a Bachelor of Science degree while I was in Seattle. I had my three-year nursing degree but I continued my education at the University of Washington. Helen, the cousin I lived with in Seattle, was an art professor at the university. We shared an apartment with her brother who was studying to be an accountant. I went to classes in the evenings when I worked days. It took a while, but the whole time I lived there, I was working toward my degree. I also partied a lot—I ran that into the ground. I met a lot of people and had wonderful experiences. One apartment I lived in was on Queen and Hill. It had a beautiful rose garden. And I've never forgotten the Easter morning that I went to sunrise services. The sun was coming up, slowly lighting the sky, the buildings, the people around me and the roses in bloom everywhere.

35

Another job I had was in a medical building in downtown Seattle. We were on the second floor above a drugstore. It was an emergency clinic. One of our main services was using leeches to clear up black eyes. I handled so many leeches that I knew exactly how to apply them and which ones would work the best. People came in with black eyes, and we'd fix them up. If I remember rightly, one black eye cost around two hundred dollars to treat back then.

Our other big business was inserting gold pessary rings into ladies of the night. The rings were used by prostitutes as a form of birth control. They were made of solid gold. I was tempted to take one and use it as jewelry. They came in all sizes and fit inside the neck of the uterus. We didn't do testing for venereal diseases, though. The prostitutes went to the police department for that. We worked three shifts at the clinic and also did minor surgery using Novocain. We stitched up anyone who came around. We even did casts for broken bones. There was an x-ray machine as well. Junior interns worked with us, and if we needed more support we just called in other medical personal to help. All sorts of characters came to the clinic. At the end of each week we were paid in cash. No taxes. Nothing. Just cash. I learned not to ask questions.

One thing that plagued me not only in Seattle but my whole life was toothaches. I always had bad teeth, and they became quite a problem when I was on my own. I'd lose time from work. I suffered from the pain they caused. The visits to the dentist to have them fixed and re-fixed ate up my money. So I made a decision. It says in the Bible, if your arm offends you, cut it off. My teeth offended me. I decided to have all my teeth pulled and get false teeth. So one weekend when I had time off from nursing, I had every last tooth pulled out. My dentist, Dr. Harrington, thought I had really lost my mind, but economically my teeth were a loss. I didn't want them any more. My friends and I had a tooth party in celebration of my liberation from my teeth. I had quite a few drinks so I didn't feel much pain. The dentist had already taken an impression and made my false teeth. I could

36

see no reason to throw money into a mouth that was always hurting me. If you can't get along with something, get rid of it, I say. I've had false teeth since I was twenty-four.

I came back to the Midwest to see my folks from time to time during my West Coast sojourn. My concept of living was very basic. I had one suitcase, and every time I moved, I took only what fit into the suitcase and left everything else behind. So I owned very little when I went from place to place.

On a visit to see my family in North Dakota, I decided to move back to St. Paul, and that is when I met my future husband, Bud. I worked at St. Luke's Hospital again for a while. By then World War II had started.

With some other nurse friends, I joined the Minnesota National Guard. Our uniforms were very good-looking. For training, I went up north that summer to Camp Ripley. My shoulder and neck got black and blue from learning to shoot a rifle. I had to shoot both standing up and lying on my stomach. I was not too successful at hitting targets, however.

We had to do about four hours a week of duty. Great emphasis was put on the threat of an air attack so we were regularly sent up to the roof of the Lowry Building in downtown St. Paul. There was always hot coffee, cocoa, and snacks to keep us nourished as we scanned the skies with binoculars. I guess we were looking for invading Japanese airplanes. Not much chance of seeing them in the middle of the Midwest.

ஓ 6 ௧

Bud

When I called my folks to tell them I had married Everett Myers, they asked me, "Which one is he?" I'd tell my folks about different men I was going with but the guys never met my family. That's me—always independent and on my own.

I met Bud, as he was called, on the sidewalk in downtown St. Paul when I was out with a group of friends. It was 1941, and he was home on leave from the Army Air Corps. Bud was a sergeant. He was also handsome, very charming and had a big, big smile. He exuded masculinity. We hit it off right away. We went out together a few times and then wrote to each other when he left. He came to St. Paul often to visit me. I have to say I enjoyed the looks of envy from other women when Bud and I were out together. Finally, we got engaged, and I went back to Missouri with him where he was stationed at a B-29 base.

My streamlined, war-time wedding: Bud picked me up at the base in a jeep. We drove into Rolla, Missouri, found a Justice of the Peace and got married. We drove back to the base. It was January 4, 1943.

Around this same time, I heard news about a nursing friend of mine I had met while working at a Los Angeles hospital. She had enlisted and gone overseas. I got word that she was killed in Europe in a bomb attack. She was in a Red Cross ambulance. I felt sad for her and her family. That was war. I had almost enlisted with her.

I worked during the war as a civilian employee of the army, going from one military base to another setting up First Aid stations for the civilian non-military employees of the bases. I also ran the First Aid stations. The first one I worked at was in Fairmont, Nebraska. Next I worked at the base in Rolla, Missouri. At these various bases I had a staff car and driver at my disposal. When employees were sick or injured, I drove out to their homes to check on them.

Missouri is famous for its red mud. I usually had strong drivers who carried me over the mud into the houses. Some of the families I visited lived in strange circumstances to my eye. This was Ozark country. It was common to find chickens roosting on the window ledges inside houses. It blew my mind. Especially when my patients had dressings I had to change. It was a problem keeping things clean. Forget about keeping things sterile!

From there we moved to Charlotte, North Carolina. Bud was transferred, and I got a transfer as well. We lived in one of the furnished older houses that were rented out to civilians. I remember that there were insects everywhere. We had to be sure to tend to the tin cans that the legs of the bed stood in. The cans were filled with insect poison. When the bugs crawled up the sides of the cans, they'd fall in and die before getting into the bed. It was a very buggy place. Every time I walked down the street I got bugs in my hair. Since I had blond hair, the bugs were easily seen and people constantly told me, "Oh, you have a bug on your head." We also had to spray regularly for termites. Fortunately, we didn't have to endure the bugs for too long.

When we lived in North Carolina, I had to deal with segregation. Public transportation was segregated. I didn't like that, so I sat in the back of the bus. The driver told me, "Lady, you come up here. Sit in the front."

I asked him why.

"You can't sit back there with those people," he replied.

"I'll sit where I want," I said. "It's a free country, and you can't tell me where to sit." I kept my seat in the back of the bus.

We had a maid who came to the apartment to help me with housework because I had a full-time job at the base. Whenever we'd get on the bus together, she'd go sit in the back of the bus. But I brought her up to the front to sit with me. The folks on the bus stared at us. Bud would get upset with me when I told him what I did.

Bud's unit was shifted from one base to another and soon we transferred back to the B-29 base at Rolla. The Boeing B-29, called the Superfortress, was a big four-engine heavy bomber, used for daytime bombing raids. It was one of the largest aircraft in the war and a really advanced bomber for its time. I learned a lot about the B-29 from the civilians who worked on them. The bomber had specialized features such as remote control machine guns and a pressurized cabin. This was the main aircraft of the U.S. firebombing campaign against Japan in the final months of the war. It was a B-29 that carried the atomic bombs that were dropped on Hiroshima and Nagasaki.

Bud was always on call. Although he was in the Air Corps, he wasn't a pilot. He was a first sergeant in intelligence. His unit had drills all the time. Someone would knock on the door of our apartment in the middle of the night. Bud would put on his uniform and leave. I never knew when he'd be back. One time, his squadron didn't show up for several days. No one would tell us anything about them. We never knew what was happening.

Finally his squadron left. I didn't know where they had gone. We weren't told anything. I was alone and on my own again. That was war. For a while I stayed in Rolla. When we lived in Charlotte, I had met a nurse from Bethesda Hospital in St. Paul who was doing the same kind of work I was. She showed up in Rolla. At that point neither of us had a job, so we both went to work for a doctor who owned and ran a hospital in the

40

Ozarks. That was quite an education. We felt we were working in another country. We were often appalled by what we encountered. The doctor had a system. Women were on the first floor of the hospital and men on the second. I was concerned because I thought there was intermingling going on. The doctor just said to tell him which patients were visiting the other floor and he'd send them home, because, "If they were well enough to be thinking that way, they were well enough to go home."

During the war years, I worked closely with others in the war effort and made a lot of friends. It was amazing the number of people I met and how we bonded so quickly. Eventually, though, I decided to go back to my family on the farm in North Dakota. I still had no idea of when I'd see Bud again. The war was hard on us all. Victory had been declared in Europe on May 8, 1945. Now the focus was on the Pacific.

Back at home in North Dakota in August of 1945, my mother and I had picked a whole batch of green beans. We were canning them when we heard the thrilling news about V-J Day and the end of the war on the radio. It was August 14 and the emperor of Japan had surrendered. I wanted to drive into town to celebrate. My mother wouldn't let me. Mother said, "Finish the green beans, Aileen." I could hear car horns blaring. The phone was ringing off the hook with people calling us wanting to know why we weren't in town celebrating. I had to tell them I couldn't come because I was canning green beans.

Only after the war ended did I find out that Bud had been sent to Guam where his intelligence job was ground support for the mission that dropped the atomic bombs on Japan.

With the war over, I joined Bud in St. Paul, and we rented and furnished an apartment on the upper floor of a duplex. I got a nursing job right away at Miller Hospital, and then I became pregnant. But by then Bud had gotten himself into trouble with an underage girl.

Marrying Bud wasn't one of my better life choices.

41

ॐ 7 ॐ

Ron's Birth

I walked into the hospital knowing the baby was coming soon. As a nurse I knew the signs. It was a dull, dark, gloomy afternoon in May. The heavy air that engulfed me as I walked to the hospital followed me up to the maternity ward. I was by myself. My husband—well, I hadn't seen him in a few days. Bud had other things to do.

I checked myself in, got into a hospital gown and set my things, including the baby clothes I brought, in the closet. I felt so down, so deserted. I had never felt that bad before. I wished I weren't around. Bud had left and here I was.

I lay on the bed. The pains were getting closer and more intense. I waited a while then called the nurse.

"Where is my doctor? This baby is coming soon," I said.

"You're fine," insisted the nurse. "I'll let the doctor know you're here."

It was about noon. This was my first child and I was filled with anticipation and a sense of excitement. Things weren't at all well between me and Bud, but I put that out of my mind. Time enough for that later. First, I had to get this baby born.

The pains were getting more intense, almost taking my breath away. I signaled for the nurse. It seemed forever before she appeared. I told her how frequent the pains were. She didn't seem to hear me, but she checked me and said she would send me to the delivery room soon. "Has the doctor come yet?" I asked the nurse taking my blood pressure.

"He'll be here shortly," she assured me.

I had worked at this hospital as a staff nurse during my pregnancy. Now here I was having my baby at the same hospital. And I was in one hell of a mess. Bud had a gambling problem and a woman problem. A week ago he had gone away in a hurry. He had gotten involved with an underage girl, so he left the state to save his hide and avoid prosecution.

They were taking me to delivery. About time. How can they cut things so close? The pains were coming every few minutes. I was beginning to feel pressure from the baby's head. Soon he or she would be out in the world.

A stab of pain made me cry out. I asked the nurse what was going on, where the doctor was, and why we weren't getting on with things. "It'll be soon," the nurse said. "I can give you something for the pain."

"This baby is coming. I want to know where my doctor is."

"He'll be here in a little while," she said.

"No little while. This baby wants to be born. I'm a nurse, you know. Get that doctor now."

"Just hold on," the nurse said. "Be patient."

Now I was getting mad. "It's not an issue of patience! I want to see your supervisor."

She left and a few minutes later returned with the supervising nurse. Before she could open her mouth, I told her I was having a baby, it wasn't waiting, and I needed to deliver now.

"Your doctor is on his way."

"Really? He's been on his way for two hours. What is going on?" I demanded.

Well, it turned out the doctor was at a conference, and they weren't going to let the baby be born until he returned. Of course, unless he was present he couldn't charge for his services. A resident doctor prevented the baby from being born by applying pressure and holding my legs closed.

"This is ridiculous," I screamed at them. "I'm having this baby now. You and I both know the consequences of what you're doing. The pain is killing me."

"The doctor will be here soon. Just hold out a bit longer," the supervisor insisted. "I'll give you something for pain."

The pain was so intense. They gave me a shot. I was furious because I knew what could happen.

Because of my small size, I feared I couldn't deliver the baby normally. I should probably have had a cesarean. But now it was too late.

The doctor finally arrived, and everyone began hurrying around. He called for the forceps. The delivery room grew very quiet. The nurses hushed each other. No one looked at me. At last my baby was born. Immediately they handed the baby to the pediatrician and nurse who worked over him frantically. I screamed at them. "I told you this would happen," I shouted over and over in fury. They rushed the baby out of the room to the nursery.

The long labor and forceps delivery caused injury to his head, and he didn't breathe for a while after being born. Oh God, I remember thinking, just take him if he isn't going to be right.

I was exhausted. I think they gave me something to make me sleep. When I woke up, it was dark. I got up and went to the nursery. There was my baby. He didn't look good. He was on oxygen.

I asked the nurse what was the matter. She mumbled something about him needing a bit of help. He seemed to be struggling to breathe, struggling to live. I wondered if I would lose him. My heart was broken. I knew this shouldn't have happened.

The next day the specialists did some tests and told me the baby had very poor motor skills, probably some brain damage, eye problems, and difficulty breathing. They walked out and left the baby with me in my arms.

I knew then that he wasn't going to be one hundred percent okay. I also knew it didn't matter. I knew I'd stay with him until the day I died—even if he was gong to be a blooming idiot.

God, just keep him alive, please.

I tried to nurse him. I had picked out the name Ron, and that's what I began calling him. As I held him and watched him struggle for breath, I said to him, "Ron, I will never leave you. If you live, I promise to be with you always. I'll help you, whatever it takes. I'll always be by your side. So help me, I will."

ဩ 8 ଔ

You Can Go Home Again

After a few days in the hospital, Ron and I went back to my apartment. I was alone, broke—I wasn't working—and I had a disabled infant to care for who was barely hanging on to life.

Bud's parents and family were always nice to me and one of his sisters stayed with me when I brought Ron home. I hardly slept. Ron's breathing was erratic, so I would keep him on my chest to monitor his breathing. When it stopped, I'd work to get him to breathe again. It went on that way for what seemed like weeks. Then my sister-in-law had to go back home. I had no support. Bud had not appeared, and I thought it was pretty clear he wasn't going to show up or send me any money. I was heartsick and alone. The first few weeks passed by in a daze of heartbreak and sleepless exhaustion.

One evening when Ron was a few weeks old, I heard the key in the lock. The door opened, and Bud walked in as if nothing had happened. "Hi, Aileen, honey."

He tried to put his arms around me. I pushed him away.

46

"Aw, Aileen, don't be sore at me. Hey, we had some good times."

"Good times don't mean anything, Bud. You were off with someone else while I was having your baby."

"But I still love you, honey."

"That's not my definition of love."

"Look, I know I made a mistake. Why don't you try to forgive me?"

"It's not about forgiveness. It's about survival. Ron's and mine. And you aren't helping. Not one bit."

"But you won't let me. Don't you see that?"

"What you did told me a lot about you. Do you see that?"

"It won't happen again. I promise. Let's get back together. Let's try to be a family, okay?"

The baby stirred in his crib and started to whimper.

"The baby's sick, huh? What's wrong with him?"

"He has a head injury, Bud, and I don't know what his future will be. I do know that he needs a lot of care." I looked at Ron then at Bud. "What will you do for us, Bud? You broke my heart. Will you break his as well? I won't let you. Just leave. Now."

"Don't do this to me, Aileen."

"Leave. You say you want to help. Are you going to give us some money? I haven't worked since the baby was born."

"I'll send you money. As soon as I get a job, I'll send money. You'll see. You'll change your mind about me."

Bud left. He never sent me a dime.

"Sue the hospital, Aileen," my friends urged me. "Get a lawyer." The day of my appointment I didn't have anyone to leave Ron with so I brought him along. I told the lawyer my story.

"You've got grounds to sue," he said. "I'd recommend that. And we'll go after your husband. Make him pay," he urged. "You can get him to come back."

"I don't want Bud back! I don't want anything to do with him," I insisted, "but I'd like some support. What are my chances?"

"I've told you what you can do. Call me when you're ready and we'll talk about how to proceed."

I thanked the lawyer. On the bus home I knew I'd never sue the hospital and even though Bud promised to send money, I felt sure I'd never see it without a fight. The lawyer said I could get a big settlement from the hospital—enough to pay for help and treatment for Ron. I'd have to sue. That meant dealing with more lawyers, court appearances, legal stuff. I'd have to fight and be tough. But I couldn't. When you're alone and brokenhearted and you have nothing, you don't have the strength to go out and attack. At least I didn't. I couldn't pay the rent on the apartment. I was stone broke. And I was caring for an infant who was struggling to live. The circumstances of my life couldn't have been worse.

Bud's father came over and helped me pack my things. Bud's sister and her husband had been living with her folks. They would take over the apartment and the furnishings. I was going back home to North Dakota. I didn't see any other way at that time.

I knew I had to take care of Ron and take care of him I would. He was the cutest little guy. A darling baby. And I loved him.

I had to take a long, hard look at my life. I felt I had done significant work for the war effort setting up the First Aid stations for civilian workers at B-29 bases. I had also worked at that hospital in the Ozarks. Before the war, when I was traveling and working on the West Coast, I followed my impulses and pretty much did what I wanted. My life was really happy. No stress, no big problems. I believed that if you did the very best possible, everything would be fine. I had a happy childhood and a good family. I had an education and a profession. Then to have all this come crashing down on me! My marriage had failed spectacularly. I couldn't work because I had to care for my disabled son. I really wasn't prepared for all the responsibility. The blow almost broke me.

In June, with Ron barely six weeks old, we rode to North Dakota with a Presbyterian minister and his daughter who were going to visit his mother. The six-hundred-mile trip to my family's home gave me lots of time for reflection. I knew that my parents would never judge me and that I could count on their unconditional love and caring. The problem was with myself. I couldn't believe what had happened. I had no idea what would become of Ron and me.

The familiar houses and landscape of my childhood brought me out of my reverie. Ron woke up as the minister pulled into the road leading to my parents' farm. They welcomed us so warmly. As I turned to wave good-bye to the minister and his daughter, I wondered how my life would turn out.

I spent over a year in North Dakota with Ron. For me, living in North Dakota was a gift from God. It made everything seem more normal. My parents' support helped me stabilize and lay the groundwork for the rest of my life. What a great gift to have had caring parents like mine. Truly, they can be called the salt of the earth. Nothing is really good without that. Mine were the most wonderful parents anyone could wish for.

"Well, Aileen," said my mother one day shortly after Ron and I arrived, "you should have some cash to use for what you need." With that she bent over and flicked back a corner of the living room carpet. Bills in various denominations were spread out flat on the floor. She picked up some and handed them to me. So this is where she stashed the money she made from her cream and butter and flowers. I had been walking over my mother's bank for years! Mother also had me visit her friend Mildred, a social worker with the county's social service department. She suggested I work as a home nursing teacher.

I was truly grateful for my education, especially for being a nurse. I had done pediatric nursing, so I felt capable of taking care of Ron. He had a choking problem when he ate. That worried my parents. They were always afraid something would happen and didn't feel they could care for him. Fortunately, the teaching job I found with the county welfare system allowed me to take Ron along while I gave demonstrations at churches and schools. I drove my dad's truck to the sessions. The classes were quite a success. "All that you need to be a good home nurse you already have in your own kitchen," I'd tell the women. What I didn't read or find in books, I invented out of my own experience. I also provided care and advice as part of my job. At least I had a little bit of money coming in. Of course, after the cost of traveling back to St. Paul to take Ron to doctors, I didn't have much money left.

While my parents were supportive of Ron and me, the attitude of some of my relatives was a shock. One of them warned me, "You'll taint the normal children by having a disabled child around." So I crossed them off my list. I simply shut out people like that, closed the door and never thought of them again. I told my mother to talk to them because I wouldn't. I couldn't lower myself to speak to people with such backward ideas.

Bud put in another appearance on Ron's first birthday. He came to North Dakota with a list of institutions in Missouri that would take disabled children. I was so mad at him. How could he suggest I abandon this cute little guy, our child?

"That way we can get back together and start all over again," he said waving the list in my face.

"Where's your car?" I asked him.

"Out front."

"Well, you get in it and get the hell out of here. Don't come and try that again."

50

❧ 9 ❧

Back to St. Paul

When Ron was about thirteen months old, my father bought me a train ticket to St. Paul so I could take Ron to a specialist at Gillette Children's Hospital. The specialist confirmed my suspicion that my son had cerebral palsy. Ron wasn't definitively diagnosed until then. Although he didn't develop the characteristic spasticity until age two, he never crawled like other babies. He couldn't hold his head up even though he could sit. His hand movements weren't too bad and he didn't have any facial grimaces. Because of the difficult birth and lack of oxygen, I knew he had suffered some brain damage, but brain injuries are difficult to diagnose. I kept hoping it would be less severe. The medical diagnosis finally confirmed his condition.

I told the doctor that I would work with Ron. I planned on devoting my entire life to helping him in every way possible. It became my total mission in life. I had only myself to rely on. I had no time for tears, only planning and action. And this mindset has continued over the years. After I got Ron's diagnosis, we took the train back to North Dakota. My plan was to return to St. Paul. My sister Ruth's in-laws, the Smiths, had a house on Seventh Street, and they offered me a room for twenty-five

51

dollars a week. They would take care of Ron while I worked. My dad gave me two hundred and fifty dollars to get started. Fortunately I found a nursing job at Miller Hospital again a few days after arriving.

We moved from place to place for several years. People were very good to us. Next we moved in with Bill and Liz Havilland on Selby Avenue. They wanted Ron to live with them. He was two by then. Liz had cosmopolitan tastes. When I saw her giving Ron a cracker with something black on it, I asked, "What's that?"

"Caviar," she told me as Ron ate it up. He liked that terrible-looking salty stuff, but it horrified me. Ron was treated to the best gourmet food. She served shrimp cocktail and caviar on Fridays. He thrived on it. I worked a late shift and came home around 11:30 P.M. to find him fast asleep snuggled up in Liz's very ample arms. "Shhh," she said. I let him spend the night. Her arms were more inviting than his crib. And she was cozy. I wasn't. I had to wrap myself up in a blanket or a robe when I held him because I was so thin. I didn't want Ron to think he had a scarecrow for a mother.

The next place we lived was at Della and Carl Poppenberger's. Della was a nurse friend of mine. They lived in a large home on Arcade Street near Tanners Lake—a truly nice family with two children, Bill and Carol. We fit in very well. It was a happy time. How lucky for both of us that Ron was surrounded during these various moves by people who loved and cared for him. We were truly blessed.

"Aileen, I noticed red spots on Ron today," said Della. "You don't think—?"

I looked at Ron and saw that he seemed to be running a fever. "I'll take him to his pediatrician tomorrow. I sure hope it's not chicken pox."

It was chicken pox and a bad case. He was developing pneumonia as well. His pediatrician was alarmed and had his assistant arrange for Ron to be admitted to Children's Hospital immediately. Della drove us to Children's. Ron was having trouble breathing and didn't look good at all. A nurse and then the doctor evaluated him. They wanted to put him in an isolation unit. There were lots of other sick children. The staff seemed so busy. They left us alone for long stretches of time. Ron had another bout of difficult breathing, and Della and I sprang into action. I sat him up and massaged his chest while Della went for the nurse. It took them a half hour to come with the oxygen. As Ron's breathing slowly returned to normal, Della and I looked at each other over Ron's head and all the machines surrounding him. "Home," I mouthed silently. Della nodded. I told the doctor we'd take our chances with him at home and left.

I held Ron tightly in my arms. He would have died there. He needed constant attention. It was lucky that both of us were nurses—it took the two of us to keep him going. One of us had to be with him at all times to make sure he kept breathing. The steamer was on so much that the wallpaper came down in the room. I can't even remember how many crises he had during that illness. We were up all hours. Together, Della and I pulled him through.

Over and over again throughout my life I reflected on how grateful I was to have my nursing profession. It sustained me and my family. It gave me the skills to help Ron survive and probably saved my father's life. Once when I was home on vacation, my father was gored by a bull. We tore up sheets to wrap around his abdomen and got him into the back of the pickup. Mother drove the truck while I rode in the back monitoring my dad's condition the twenty-one miles to the hospital. Our neighbor had called to say we were coming so when we arrived, he immediately went into surgery. He lost a part of his intestine, but surprisingly there wasn't more damage. I was so grateful for my nursing skills that time.

Nursing also gave me many opportunities all throughout my life to work with people, to make a difference, and to truly help others. Often when I finished the night shift at the hospital, I'd sit in the cafeteria drinking coffee to get the strength to drive home. I had a lot of heartache in those years. But I never looked back. Good thing I didn't. I would have gone nuts.

I remember my work in the Emergency Room. I felt so sad witnessing the tragic results of careless driving. Beautiful young people all smashed up and quite often dead from head injuries. Everyone working there gave them the best care they could. I also worked in intensive care where I had to keep fourteen IVs running at one time.

At the other extreme was what we called the Gold Coast—the fifth floor of Miller Hospital. People who could afford it came in to rest a bit and be pampered. Each afternoon there was a happy hour. Trays were set up and zipped about with whatever they desired. Patients provided their own alcohol, but we served it up. They even had guests in. I laughed to myself. I figured I was contributing to the health of our local economy.

Miller Hospital had a special reputation as a place for the wealthy and for members of "old St. Paul" society to go to for their medical care and, yes, they received certain privileges. In some ways Miller was like a fine hotel for patients with means. Ample suites, Limoges china, fresh game and fish, champagne and cocktails, and adjacent rooms rented for maids were all part of a wealthy patient's stay. But the high fees they paid covered the free beds the hospital was committed to providing for the poor. There was no welfare or medical assistance back then, so private hospitals themselves covered the costs of a certain number of "free beds" and that included all the medical care such patients required. City and county hospitals also took in many of the sick who were unable to pay. Health insurance plans such as the Blue Cross Plan of Minnesota were just being introduced at this time.

To make extra money, I had started working weekends at 3M—Minnesota Mining and Manufacturing Company—on the eastside of St Paul, but I still couldn't cover all of our expenses. I decided I had to get child support from

Ron's father to help pay for Ronnie's care. I knew Bud was living in Kansas City and working for an insurance company. I wanted the county attorney to pick Bud up and bring him back here for trial.

Several times a week, after I got off work, I'd take Ron with me and go downtown to the courthouse. I had spoken to Mr. James Lynch, the county attorney, but he never did anything. I suppose he looked at me and saw a woman with an education and a profession who was decently dressed, so he must have figured I could take care of myself. He didn't seem to be in any hurry to bring Bud back. After the first time I spoke with him, I could never get in to see Mr. Lynch again. His secretary always told me he was in court, at a meeting, out of town. I was really disgusted. So one day I stopped over at the *St. Paul Pioneer Press* newspaper office and told them about the trouble I was having getting the county attorney to bring back my husband for support money. I explained that I was a single mother and needed money for childcare and orthopedic treatments for Ron. "Would you take a photo of us?" I asked. A photographer snapped shots of Ron and me standing in front of the courthouse.

Again I approached the secretary and asked to see Mr. Lynch.

"He's in a conference. I can't bother him," she said.

I had Ron in one arm. I marched across the room and opened his door. He was sitting at his desk alone.

"Mr. Lynch, I've been coming to your office for weeks now," I reminded him. "All I want is for you to bring my husband back and order him to pay us support money. You're running for another term. I've contacted the newspaper. If you don't bring him back for trial, the *Pioneer Press* is coming over to write a story about how you aren't doing anything for the people who elected you. They've already got a photo of my son and me waiting in front of the courthouse."

"Now, now, let's talk this over calmly," he said.

That was on a Thursday. The arrest warrant was issued, and by Monday Bud was in court in St. Paul. He was ordered to pay us eighty dollars a month. Bud had to go into the reserves in order to earn the money for child support payments.

Mr. Lynch may have ignored me because I had a job, didn't look destitute, and always dressed as best I could. But he didn't know who he was dealing with. Yes, it was blackmail, but I got him to act.

I had help during this time from a wonderful attorney, Stan, the husband of Julie, my friend from nurses' training. He got a kick out of the whole business with Mr. Lynch.

After I started receiving support from Bud, I had enough money to rent our own apartment. I found a place on lower Summit Avenue across from Miller Hospital where I was working. It was great. It was the first time I ever really had my own space in all those years. Now Ron and I lived a bit better. The apartment had an enclosed porch that I used as a second bedroom for a live-in helper. Our first helper was Margaret. She lived with us on weekdays and had weekends off. Margaret was a wonderful, kind person who had many years of experience with children. She was very devoted to Ron. She was with us for a long time. She took care of Ron and made meals for us during the work week. I paid her the eighty dollars monthly child support money. Imagine trying to do that nowadays.

We got our first pet that Easter. It was a little white bunny rabbit. Ron was so thrilled with it. He loved to hold and pet his white bunny. At night we put the bunny into its cage. He had the run of the apartment during the day. I didn't think at the time that it would grow into a huge rabbit. I knew rabbits could be trained, but all the time we had him I could never figure out where the bunny did his business.

On weekends when Margaret was off and I was working the extra job at 3M, I'd take Ron to work with me. He had a tricycle that we fixed up especially for him, and he would cruise around the lobby of the building where I worked. The folks at 3M were very good to us.

Soon I was offered a full-time position as an industrial nurse at 3M. I made less money, but I had complete medical insurance that covered both Ron and me. Up to that time Ron and I had lived in rooms and apartments. Now I was determined to have a house with a yard. I found a nice upper duplex on George Street on the West Side. Mary and Joe Ippolita owned the place and lived downstairs. They were very kind to us. I looked forward to moving. The folks at 3M made hot dishes for a moving party and lots of people came over to help us move.

That day I found out where Ron's bunny rabbit had been doing his business. He used the back of the TV cabinet the entire time we had him.

❧ 10 ☙

My True Blue Crosley

The city of St. Paul had a great streetcar system, and I rode the street-cars regularly, but it was hard to get around with Ron because of his cerebral palsy. I was working at Miller Hospital and decided I needed a car. I spotted one that I thought would be perfect for Ron and me in the display window at Lexington Motors on University Avenue and fell in love with it. The car was a Crosley. A small blue Crosley. There isn't such a car anymore, but maybe with smaller cars coming back for economic and environmental reasons, we might see something like it again.

I loved that car—but I didn't have the money to buy it. At the dealership, they told me I could have the car but had to sell a certain number of cars for them. So I did. I sold six cars and that paid for my car. The price back then was about three hundred fifty dollars. People saw me driving it and asked me about the car. They decided it was a perfect second car for running errands. I'd take them for a ride in my Crosley and drive them straight over to Lexington Motors to buy one for themselves.

At that time, we all knew the Crosley name. Powel Crosley, Jr., was a successful businessman and inventor who started an auto accessory company then set his sights on producing inexpensive but high quality radios. He made radios accessible to millions of people, and in 1922 he opened Cincinnati radio station WLW so people would have something to listen to on their new Crosley radios! By the thirties, he and his brother Lewis were also making refrigerators and other electrical appliances. He is credited with the idea of putting shelves for food in the refrigerator door—voila!—the "Shelvadore."

Apparently Crosley then decided to do for the automobile what he had done for radio. He aimed for the low-priced mini-car niche in the United States. In the late thirties, his company began producing two-cylinder cars that weighed less than a thousand pounds. He even sold the cars through Macy's department store!

When World War II broke out, the company's attention turned to manufacturing vehicles for the war. At the same time, however, gas rationing made the little cars attractive to own. After the war, Crosley Motors brought out two-door sedans, a convertible, and pickup trucks. Station wagons, the first American postwar sports car called the Hotshot, and a 1950 Crosley Super Sports model with leopard skin seats all came off the production line along with my Crosley sedan.

My car was bright blue, so I painted the wheel spokes bright red. No leopard skin upholstery in my car. Instead I made red and white polka dot slipcovers for the seats. I often stopped by an odds-and-ends fabric shop where cloth was sold by the pound from bins. When I saw that snappy red polka dotted fabric, I bought it for my Crosley.

I felt pretty good having my own car. Ronnie and I (I'm fairly small) fit into it just right. It had two front seats and a bench in back. My Crosley was smaller than a VW bug. We could put lunch on its roof and eat off it standing up. I had a special red-checkered tablecloth that I used on it for our picnics.

The sub-compact car was so tiny and sat so low to the ground that I needed a periscope especially when I came up to corners. I'd inch up to an intersection ever so slowly. As soon as the way was clear, I'd scoot around the corner real fast. The car didn't have turn signals, so I drew a skull and covered it with some 3M reflective tape and put it on the end of a stick. When I wanted to make a turn, I pushed it out the window.

The guys I worked with at Minnesota Mining and Manufacturing would have fun with my Crosley, especially those on the three-to-eleven evening shift. They'd pick up my car and put it up on the steps of the minerals building, Building 12, where I worked as a nurse. Or someone would crawl underneath and hold on to it so I couldn't move after starting it. A few times they picked it up, brought it inside and set it in the lobby. When I finished the evening shift at 3M, I was never sure where I'd find my car.

If there was a lot of snow and the roads were bad, I just drove it on the sidewalk. Fortunately, people generally did a nice job of shoveling. The car, however, didn't have a window defroster—an essential item for driving during Minnesota winters. But one engineer at 3M fixed up a wooden box with a fan and wires that plugged into the cigarette lighter. That worked fine.

One Christmas I decided to go to North Dakota with Ron, who was about four then, to spend the holidays with my family. I heard a storm was coming, but it looked nice out, so I started driving. I had made the trip before in my little blue Crosley, and I knew the way. We got all the way to Grand Forks on the Minnesota-North Dakota border. When we left Grand Forks, it still didn't look bad. I had about two hundred more miles to go to my parents' home in Towner. But soon I was driving through blowing snow, and then the storm hit. It was a bad one. The snow was coming down fast and heavy. The snow was so thick that soon I couldn't see the road. In order not to go into the ditch on the highway, I had to get out of the car and walk ahead clearing the snow from the road and marking the path. I'd get back in the car and drive where I had cleared the snow. Then I'd repeat the procedure. It was very frightening. I did some loud praying. I could imagine being lost and dying on the road with the baby. Ron was next to me and there was a heater in the car, but it was getting dark fast.

I decided to look for a house and ask to stay until the storm passed. I found a road that I thought must lead to a farmhouse, so I pulled off the highway and began inching my way along the road. There was a light on the right hand side of the road. I left the car with the motor running and walked down to the ditch and found a way to run toward it. Then the light went out but I kept on running. I saw the light again. It was from a truck. They were out checking on the livestock at a feeding station. I don't know how the people in the truck saw me, but they did. I got into the truck. I was crying. They drove to my car and pulled it to the farmhouse a few miles further on. We finally got into the warm, safe house. The family took such good care of us. They fed us and gave me a hot whiskey to calm me down. Then Ron and I crawled into a big feather bed and slept soundly.

Of course, my own family was frantic. My mother told me, "I'll never forget the night you didn't show up with that baby." The phone at the farmhouse didn't work, so I couldn't call my parents that night. The next day my rescuers went to call my folks and tell them we were safe. They had been up all night worried to death about us. Ron and I stayed a few days with the family because we had to wait until the roads were plowed to drive the rest of the two hundred miles home.

My mother sent a thank you letter to the family.

The people who took me in said, "You must be crazy. Do you always do crazy things like this?"

I told them that I had taken the six hundred-mile trip in the car before and had been fine. But despite my spunky attitude, I knew I had put us in danger. I've come so close to having serious things happen to me, it's a wonder I'm still alive. But I'll probably just die in bed not doing anything interesting or dangerous at all. I often wonder how I survived. God must have had other plans. Sometimes I just wonder about that.

Eventually I had to let my Crosley go. I couldn't get tires for it anymore. The company closed in 1952, and the tires on my car wore out. They were small and thin, more like those of a big bicycle. I had the car for a long time. It was such a reliable car.

The American love affair with big cars drove the Crosley out of the market despite many innovations in automotive design such as a 1949 venture with four-wheel disc brakes. However, Crosley engines were used in boats and other small vehicles for decades.

The next car I owned was a Henry J. Kaiser—the Henry J. It was brown and had wings in the back that came way up. You'd swear to God it looked part airplane.

I not only do weird things, I drive weird cars.

❧ 11 ❧

Explosion at 3M

I looked at Ron still asleep in his crib as I put on my crisp white nurse's uniform and pinned on my nurse's cap. Margaret, the woman who took care of Ron, would get him up and feed him while I was at work at Minnesota Mining and Manufacturing Company. It was barely light out as I drove my blue Crosley the few miles to the plant that Thursday morning, February 8, 1951.

As an industrial nurse at 3M, I worked in the medical department of Building 12, the large minerals building where abrasives and coatings for products like sandpaper were prepared. There was also a nurse in the nearby tape building, but that day I was the only nurse on duty in our department. The charge nurse, whose station was my building, had taken medical leave that week. I sat at a desk right inside the door under a big clock on the north wall and signed in employees who where coming back from medical leave. The first person I signed in was a supervisor.

"George, you're back already. How are you feeling?"

"The doctor says I'm okay."

"You should have taken a few more sick days off. You could go ice fishing," I joked as I signed him in.

"No, not me," he said. "I really missed all my co-workers. I have a great time at work."

What a fine person, I thought to myself. He's always so upbeat and positive.

I had gotten up from the desk and was walking across the room to the door when I felt a tremendous jolt. The clock by the desk fell off the wall. There was a rumbling sound. Then I heard a deafening explosion and the sound of crashing concrete and metal. People started screaming. Dust was billowing all around. It was eerie and unreal. I groped my way to the phone and called the emergency number. When I got the operator I said, "There has been a terrific explosion here. There are many people hurt. Send several ambulances."

I turned back to the scene around me. Pandemonium prevailed. The guards had grabbed stretchers and had run into the corridor to help the wounded, but people were crowding and pushing in panic and yelling conflicting orders. Many were bleeding and looked dazed. Some were screaming from pain and fear.

"Follow me," I shouted to the guards. "We have to walk slowly and in a line." I realized it was up to me to control the panic. I went ahead of the team. I knew the injured would identify me in my white uniform. We headed right into the thick of the heavy dust and the crowd of wounded and bleeding victims. When people saw us moving resolutely, they calmed down. We were able to assist the injured and locate those who had been killed.

The first fatality I saw was George, the supervisor I had just signed in.

The guards got several injured men onto stretchers and carried them out to the ambulances. They brought a young man who had been injured into the medical area and set him on the floor. His name was Otto. I knew that because his name was embroidered on his shirt. He wasn't a 3M employee. He had been making a delivery that morning.

"Nurse, can you find my boots?" he asked me as I attended to him. "My boots are brand new. I just bought them yesterday at Sears."

"Yes, I'll find them for you," I assured him.

Both of Otto's feet had been blown off. We did what we could to stop the bleeding. I held his hand as they put him on a stretcher to take him to an ambulance. I later heard he died on the way to the hospital.

"Nurse, there are people behind that wall. You're small. Crawl through this hole and see if they're alive or dead," one of the guards said.

I looked at the jagged edges of the gaping hole blown in the wall. I could hear the cries of injured men. "Give me a hand." They assisted me as I squeezed through and stepped onto a pile of rubble and dust on the other side. While they made the hole bigger, I helped a few injured men closer to the hole so they could be put on stretchers. The dust was still thick and gritty. Other victims were trapped behind machinery or under concrete slabs, and we couldn't reach them without heavy moving equipment.

The blast had blown out the main elevator. We went down the stairway and found two people there. But we couldn't get the stretchers around the corners, so they had to be carried up the stairs to the stretchers.

There seemed to be so many injured. It was horrible. I tried to assess each one and act quickly. I applied pressure bandages and did whatever I could to stop the bleeding on those who had lost limbs. There were others we couldn't save.

At some point I realized the cries of pain and confusion had stopped. The shouts for help and the barked commands had ceased. Now there were only clusters of company personnel conferring with fire and police officials. I stood in the dust-laden disaster area. My uniform was a strange shade of gray with splotches of blood and grime. I was covered with dust. When I spoke, I could taste grit on my lips.

"Things are under control," a manager said to me. "We're closing the plant. Everyone's leaving. You should go to the hospital to be checked."

I nodded and said good-bye to the guards who had worked so hard. Then I got in my car and drove home. I wanted to get away from it all. I wanted to see Ron. I also wanted to get cleaned up and wash my hair.

Margaret gasped when she saw me, then told me to call my folks immediately. My mother had called. She had heard on the news in North Dakota that a nurse at 3M was killed in the blast. They thought I was dead. Margaret had been frantic hearing the reports on the radio.

I listened to the news. There had been one large explosion, and it had blown out the elevators and wall on the west side of our building. Eleven people died and fifty-nine had been injured. Those of us who survived had mineral dust in our lungs. Friends said I could have sued for the trauma and all that mineral dust. I didn't. I just went back to work when the plant opened the following week, glad to be there.

The families of those who had been killed were each assigned a 3M executive who helped them and made sure their expenses were met. Mr. Carlton, the president of 3M, called me at home just as I was trying to wash all the mineral dust out of my hair. "Please take some time off from work," he said. "I think you should stay home. This has been a dreadful experience for all of us."

"No," I said. "I'll be back on duty when the plant opens."

Thinking about this, I realize I must have had my brains addled by the explosion to refuse time off with pay!

It took four washings to get all the dust and grit out of my hair.

It took many months to wash away the pain and sadness I felt.

ᔆ 12 ᩃ

Lindsay School and Petey

I meant it when I asked God to keep Ron alive and said, "No matter what, I'll stay with him until the day I die—even if he's gong to be a blooming idiot." That's been the basis for my life. Having that responsibility made me grow up real fast. Everything I did after that had to be centered on Ron and his care. It's as if we jumped into life in tandem, and he depended on me to guide him to a safe landing just as I depended on my wonderful skydiving guide, Kerry McCauley, to bring me through the sky and back to earth. Funny, isn't it? Or maybe curious. My son has been the main ingredient in my variegated life, as I call it. He certainly expanded my heart and my mind and my life in unexpected ways.

He also drove me crazy more times than I care to remember. As a little guy he was amazingly cute and clever. He worked so hard at his therapy and never seemed to tire of it or complain. Basically, he always believed he'd get better and better. I taught him that he was as good as anyone else.

The doctor at Gillette Children's Hospital, who confirmed the cerebral palsy diagnosis when Ron was thirteen months old, gave me a complete set of exercises and a prescription for leg braces that Ron had to wear at night to keep his leg muscles stretched. We got those at Gillette as well. Ron and I did the exercises daily. He needed the stretching and strength building to keep up his range of motion and muscle tone. We hoped he'd be able to walk one day and, if he did, it would be a direct result of our exercise routine.

On weekdays we'd usually exercise before dinner. I'd start by having Ron lie on the floor, and we'd play reach and stretch.

"Ronnie, can you kick the ball? Good!" I'd move his ball a little farther away each time. Sometimes he'd whack it across the room and laugh as I chased the ball. To strengthen his muscles, I had him push against my hands. We didn't have clever devices like ankle weights back then. Instead I put old bath towels to creative uses. To finish our session, I tied a towel around his waist and held onto it. "That's right—up on your knees. Now what can you do? I'm holding you. Can you go to your ball?" He tried to figure out how to get around on his knees.

With my help, Ron eventually was able to stand. I'd move along on my knees holding him up with my hands, and he'd try taking steps. Although he could walk with someone supporting him, I saw that he really wanted to walk on his own. Again, I'd hold him from behind by the bath towel around his waist and he'd concentrate on convincing first one foot then the other to lift, come forward, and set down.

I noticed that I had to provide the verbal stimulus to his walking. "Walk. Walk. Lift your foot. Move it forward. Step down on it. Walk. Can you say that too?" The minute I stopped speaking to him, he fell. It's a head-to-foot connection—patterned walking. I had read about patterned walking and thought it was astonishing. In fact, from the time Ron was born, I read every psychology book I could on the power of the mind and on the mental stimulus needed to perform an action. My reading convinced me that you can do amazing things with your mind.

I have to give Ron a lot of credit for his hard work and persistence. We could see the progress he made week by week. Ron's exercise routine was also carried out by the women I hired to help us.

68

Ronnie, as we sometimes called him, never tired of trying to help himself. Sometimes it almost broke my heart. He also had a speech problem, and so we had sessions with a speech therapist. I'd work at home with him on his pronunciation. Ron never stopped trying to talk correctly. He asked, "Do I do right?" so many times. All these exercises and drills had to be done on a daily basis, yet it wasn't tiresome. I found such deep joy in every little thing he accomplished in his world. Our daily sessions were a close and happy time. Ron always had a great smile despite the hard things we did.

Petey, our parakeet, supervised Ron's exercise sessions. He would choose a perch close to Ronnie and watch us. Petey had the run of the place. When we first got him, we tried to keep him in a cage, but Petey would have none of that. After a week with us, he was flying free around the apartment. His roosting perch was in one room, his mirror and food stand and toys were in another.

Petey was a beloved member of our small family. He would sit on Ronnie's head, and the two of them would watch TV together. When Ron tried to walk, Petey would cling to Ron's hair, holding on tight because it wasn't a smooth ride. When it got too rough, Petey would take off. He circled back to his perch on Ron's head when he could. At night I'd check on Ron asleep and often find Petey sitting on the headboard watching him.

Ron took his first steps when he was four. I have pictures of him walking alone alongside a bench in Como Park. "See, I'm good," Ron would say when he was walking. His grandparents took turns coming to see him. They were devoted to Ron. He always tried so hard to show them he was getting better.

At age five, like all kids, Ron went off to school. I was pleased to see how well he could get around. The first school he enrolled in was the Lindsay School for Crippled Children in St. Paul. "Crippled" was the term in use then. The school was exclusively for disabled children. In addition to their classes, the children went to physical therapy at the school. Regular public schools didn't offer the accessibility, personnel, classes, or support that disabled kids receive there today.

Lindsay School was a wonderful place with fine people who were totally committed to these children. The principal, a very dedicated and resourceful lady, was assisted by a wonderful staff. Ron had a teacher who was really special, Beverly Lewis—truly sent from God. She made all the children feel so welcomed and cared for. We kept in touch with her and some of the others for many years. They lived their lives helping disabled kids. The other parents and I could feel the affection of the staff for the children they worked with. From time to time, I'd have the teachers or the kids and their parents over to my apartment. I always went out of my way to make friends with the folks at Ron's schools to help build relationships for him.

On one occasion I had invited Ron's teachers from Lindsay School for dinner. I had made a crown roast that I was very proud of. The roasted meat sat in a circle of bones, the tips of which were covered with paper "panties" as I called them, but they were more like little chefs' hats. Sculpted mashed potatoes surrounded the roast. I placed my marvelous creation on the table and started to call everyone in to eat. Suddenly Petey flew right through the mashed potatoes and landed on one of the bones where he surveyed his contribution to the dinner. I chased him into the bathroom and shut the door. I quickly cleaned up the potatoes and mounded them up again and sprinkled paprika over it all while the guests sat with Ron in the living room. Then I called everyone in to eat. I never said a word. Everyone enjoyed their Petey-blessed potatoes and no one reported any unusual ailments.

Ron went on to first grade and learned to read, but because of muscle control difficulties with his hands, it was hard for him to write. Yet he would tell me that he felt sorry for the kids without arms or legs. Some kids used homemade carts for mobility. One little boy got around by lying down on his cart and pushing it with his arms. This was before specially designed orthopedic equipment and motorized wheelchairs. Ron moved about on his knees but also used a small walker to get around.

It's very hard for children who are disabled to get to know people. They aren't on their own enough to build rapport. Usually others are present. It occurred to me that we don't take the time to really listen to a disabled person. The rest of us move too fast. Disabled people come up against this over and over. Ron had one good friend at Lindsay. His name was Joel. It was a happy situation for both of them. I have pictures of them at a birthday party in the apartment. It was great to see the change in Ron when he had someone his own age to relate to after having had only adults for friends.

All the parents of kids with cerebral palsy at Lindsay School formed a very tight-knit and resourceful group of people who were deeply concerned about their children's welfare. We met to discuss our similar problems. The Lindsay School brought together parents of a certain type—those who kept their special needs children at home and were willing to invest time and money to support them. We had numerous fundraisers and hosted dinners that were open to the public. These brought in much-needed money to buy equipment for the school and also raised public awareness about the needs of children with cerebral palsy. CP was not spoken of very often or very openly back then.

The dedicated parents at Lindsay School advocated for children with cerebral palsy and founded the Cerebral Palsy Organization of Greater St. Paul. For a time we met in the Wilder Building on Pleasant Avenue. Later we held meetings at the Pioneer Building downtown and Neighborhood House on the West Side, and then at 991 Selby Avenue where workshops for handicapped children were started. At these work places, older kids were taught skills and were paid for the work they did.

In 1954 we became part of the national United Cerebral Palsy Association and often joined forces with the Cerebral Palsy Organizations of Greater Minneapolis and of Minnesota to work on the yearly telethon fundraiser. Ron participated in a lot of them along with other children with CP. I didn't like the idea. I thought this exploited the kids and

71

exposed them to misunderstanding, but I went along with it. Both Ron and Joel seemed to enjoy appearing in a 1954 telethon with film actor Pat O'Brien as master of ceremonies. The well known Irish actor played the lead in *Knute Rockne, All American*. Two of his later films were *The Last Hurrah* and *Some Like It Hot*. I had met him years ago when I was working in Los Angeles as a nurse. He acted like he remembered me!

Telethons were a popular form of fundraising in the fifties. That one lasted sixteen hours and featured a stream of singers, actors, dancers, and local celebrities along with the kids, their teachers and therapists all participating to raise money. That year we raised $121,000 in direct donations and pledges. Many people, especially couples, worked endlessly on fundraisers and other projects to help the kids gain recognition and demonstrate their abilities despite the effects of cerebral palsy. Before that, most of these children were simply warehoused in institutions. What a terrible loss that was! None of the people from the Lindsay School Parents group put their kids in institutions.

The way kids with disabilities are treated has changed radically. Many children, for example, used to be sent to Cambridge State School and Hospital north of the Twin Cities. It was primarily for people with epilepsy, but in 1949 they began accepting residents with developmental disabilities who generally remained institutionalized for life. Back then, rehabilitation and integration into society were not options. For a child to be "sent up to Cambridge" was disastrous. Parents got rid of the kids they didn't want. They'd drug them, bring them in and say "Look, we can't do anything with this child," and leave them there. In the early sixties, the population at Cambridge reached over two thousand.

It wasn't until the late sixties that the Minnesota Department of Public Welfare began developing treatment and rehabilitation programs. In a 1974 lawsuit involving Cambridge, the judge ruled that people with disabilities living in institutions had rights. As a result, changes led to better treatment and care, integration into general society, as well as to educational programs to encourage the development of the each individual's potential.

I can't count the times people urged me to put Ron in a home. "Home" was the euphemism for an institution, a warehouse. I could never do that. It would have been a death sentence. In order for Ron to survive and have a meaningful life, I knew he would need a lot of one-on-one attention and therapy that he'd never get in an institution. He had to be taught to sit up and to speak. He needed daily exercise. He couldn't even crawl. He had no coordination with his arms although he could get around on his knees.

But I knew he had a right to whatever help he needed to become as independent and self-sufficient as possible. It's a God-given right that each and every child should get the best care available. Thank heavens we are becoming more kind and humane as a society, with a deepening understanding of the needs and rights of disabled people, and we are seeing to it that they are given the necessary help to live as fully as possible. So many have the ability to succeed and become great people. There are many ways to have a fulfilling life. Ron was a smiling, happy child. He was always upbeat. Maybe I instilled in him my philosophy of looking ahead and not dwelling on the negative. I believe that parents do form their children's outlook on life. Creating a positive, happy outlook is our gift to them regardless of their physical problems.

The whole group of kids that went to Lindsay School with Ron is probably still alive. They would be in their fifties and early sixties now. I used to have the mothers out to my house every few years. We formed such strong bonds and really supported each other and our kids, and we made a difference in how they were able to live their lives.

One of the members of our group at Lindsay School had built a special play table for his grandson. When the little boy died, the family gave the table to Ron. This was a wonderful gift. At that time the only special equipment for kids with disabilities was homemade. I went to their house with a trailer to haul it home. It caused quite a sensation. People applauded me as I drove by. The table was huge, bigger than my car—

73

as big as a kitchen table. It was a wonderful device. The mesh seat supported Ron upright and could be adjusted so his feet touched the floor.
The circular table had padded bumpers all the way around so toys
wouldn't fall off. Yet, you could tip the table so that if Ron threw a ball,
it would roll back. We had it in the apartment for several years. Ron was
able to play at his table for long stretches of time. It made life much hap-
pier for him and he really used it a lot. When other children came over,
he could play and interact with them better sitting at his table. These little things mean so much to children like him. It seems to me that a very
special angel was always around to protect us.

When it came time to move to our new place on George Street, we
bought a cage for Petey and kept him in it after we moved. But Petey
wasn't happy. One day we found that he had simply died. I held his life-
less body while Ron petted him. "We killed Petey," Ronnie said tearful-
ly, "We put him in a cage and we killed him, didn't we?"

ༀ 13 ༁

Baltimore Rehab for Little Daniel Boone

I was always trying to figure out the best things to do for Ron. He was eager to get better, and he tolerated therapy so well. His attitude motivated me to keep searching for ways to help him gain as much mobility and independence as possible.

Of course I wondered, as any mother would, what the future held in store for him. I had no idea. And all I could do was take each day as it came in the same way he took each step that was in front of him—as best he could.

I had heard about an internationally known center for cerebral palsy in Baltimore, Maryland, the Children's Rehabilitation Institute founded by Dr. Winthrop M. Phelps. It was the only facility in the United States that offered full treatment for children with CP. Despite the costs of travel and treatment, I really wanted Ron to be seen by specialists there. The first time I took him, Ron was about six years old. We met with Dr. Phelps himself, who dedicated his life to studying and working to help children with this crippling condition. Everyday he saw and treated children from all over the world. Dr. Phelps and the CRI changed the perception and treatment of cerebral palsy worldwide.

Originally called Little's Disease (it was first described by Dr. William Little in 1843), cerebral palsy is a non-progressive condition usually caused by a brain malformation or injury before, during, or after birth. A person with any of the various manifestations of the condition was often called a "spastic," a term that is more correctly used for one of the six types of cerebral palsy that Dr. Phelps identified. In fact, it was Dr. Phelps who promoted the use of the term "cerebral palsy" to focus on the motor handicap involved and separate it from mental retardation. He recognized that, with training and help, many CP children could become contributing members of their communities. Since 1937, the CRI functioned as a residential school and clinic for children and a training center for physicians and therapists.

In the early sixties, through a joint venture of CRI and Johns Hopkins University, the John F. Kennedy Institute for the Habilitation of the Mentally and Physically Handicapped Child was established. Two decades later it became the Kennedy Krieger Institute in honor of long-time supporter Zanvyl Krieger. The Phelps Center for Cerebral Palsy and Neurodevelopmental Medicine is a part of the Kennedy Krieger Institute.

Each child is so different with respect to the causes and complications of cerebral palsy. The full extent of a child's condition was usually assessed at age two. I had a nurse friend, Irene, who lived in Arlington, Virginia. Her son Steve, two years older than Ron, also had cerebral palsy. She had taken him to the Children's Rehabilitation Institute and was very impressed. I had her set up an appointment for us.

We flew to Washington, DC on a commercial flight. At that time, the American frontiersman Daniel Boone was popular with kids. Ronnie had asked me for a Daniel Boone outfit so that's what I dressed him in for the trip, complete with the fake coonskin cap. Would you believe that a lady on the flight criticized me? "Why is he dressed in that outfit? You shouldn't draw attention to a child like that."

"My child," I told her, "has the right to enjoy the same things that other kids enjoy." When he wasn't wearing his Daniel Boone outfit, he'd wear a suit and a small-sized fedora with a snap-brim.

Irene picked us up at the airport, and we stayed at her home. Steve's cerebral palsy affected him only on one side. His speech was very clear but slow, and I could understand everything he said. Steve went to a regular school. Irene and I had many long discussions during that and subsequent visits. It was comforting for me to have a friend who faced the same challenges as I did.

Irene drove us to Baltimore to meet with the Dr. Phelps. I was really very worried. First, what would he tell me about Ron and his chances for improvement? Dr. Phelps was the first real cerebral palsy specialist to see Ron. Second, just how expensive was this going to be and could we afford it? At that point I only had my salary and what Bud sent. There wasn't much left over. This last worried me the most. I had heard that the fee for the consultation was a dollar per minute and, in addition, there would be the expense of any orthopedic equipment Ron might need. I was prepared to work the rest of my days to pay off the bill.

We had a two-hour appointment with Dr. Phelps. He was a stately, friendly man who I instinctively knew would help. He told me so much and gave me extra literature to read. That made me feel good. I sensed that I was on the right track and that I was doing what Ron needed. The doctor prescribed special braces for Ron's legs. I was pleased with all we accomplished for Ron.

Then came the hard part. "Doctor, I know this consultation is expensive, but it's worth it. I can't pay you all at once. But I will pay it all if we can set up a payment plan."

Dr. Phelps answered, "No, that's not possible."

I nearly collapsed. What was I going to do, I wondered.

Then Dr. Phelps asked me, "Do you have a dollar bill with you?"

I looked in my purse. "Yes," I answered.

"Take it out and give it to me."

I did.

"Thank you. You're paid in full," he said.

It took a moment to realize what he had done. I cried as I thanked him.

"I have faith in you and the love you have for your little boy," he said.

"You know I'll follow all your recommendations," I told him.

"I'm sure of it," he replied.

He was such a fine man and accomplished great things through his lifelong dedication to children with cerebral palsy. He helped us so much. I also heard from other parents how he brought hope, happiness, and accomplishment to the lives of many children and their families.

Dr. Phelps then sent us to the Henderson Brace Shop in Baltimore where Ron was measured for braces, extensions, and special shoes. This was literally a big step forward for Ron. Now he could walk much better. I was able make affordable payments to the brace shop. The people there were kind and supportive.

Ron and I spent a few days visiting the sights in Washington and Baltimore. I counted each day as a blessing. It seemed that around every corner we found evidence of the power of brotherly love.

I felt we were very lucky, first to have a friend to stay with on our trips to Baltimore who drove us around like visiting royalty, and then to have this arrangement with the clinic. I knew we'd have to make return trips as Ron grew and needed new braces and special shoes. But again we were lucky. Eventually, the insurance from my job at 3M covered Ron's expenses. A few times we took the train and other times we flew on the 3M Company plane. The executives were wonderful to us. After our visit to the clinic was over, we'd wait to be advised when the plane was making a return trip to the Twin Cities, then drive out to the airport to board the company plane. They did a lot of nice things for us at 3M.

We went back and forth a total of five or six different times to see Dr. Phelps. The payoff was that Ron was able to walk alone without crutches. He hated the awkward way he walked and that he often fell. In many respects it wasn't a happy life for him, but at least he had some mobility despite his way of walking.

I appreciated our stay with Irene and especially having someone to talk to about Ron. One of the things we talked about several times was sterilization. She declared her intention to sterilize her son when he reached adulthood. I was stunned. "There's no way I could do that," I told her. "It seems unjust to me. A person with a disability has so much taken away already. Why take away their fertility? No, I couldn't do that."

"But, Aileen," my friend countered, "you have to be realistic. I know that my son, no matter how much he might be able to do, will never be in a position to raise a child. Why create problems for him?"

No, I told her. I would never do that. No matter what the consequences, I assured her.

ᴓ 14 ᴔ

"You Go Be My Daddy?"

I was still young—in my thirties—and men asked me out. I had all sorts of dates. I've forgotten most of the guys I went out with, but there was one man who owned a house on Lake of the Isles, a luxury neighborhood in Minneapolis. He would have fabulous parties, and I'd be his hostess. He asked me to marry him. But I could hardly bear kissing him. How could I stand to sleep with him!

One guy—I met him when he was visiting a sick relative at the hospital—invited me to dinner. "That's fine," I said, "but we have to take my child along. That's the way it goes. I work all day and I don't get a chance to spend time with him. I'm not going to run around at night and not see him."

My friends thought I was nuts and advised me not to take Ron along on my dates. But if I wanted to go out, I had to take Ron because I didn't have a babysitter. I think I had so many boyfriends because I told them I wasn't looking to get married. It was surprising—I promised I wasn't going to snag them and we'd go out have a good time. Of course, when they came to my house, Ronnie would always ask them, "You go be my daddy?" I trained him to do that, but I'd tell the guys I hadn't.

"What did he say?"

80

"Ask him."

"What did you say, little fellow?"

"You go be my daddy?"

Then I'd tell the guy, "Okay, there's the door. You can run out right now."

One fellow took me dancing at the Nicollet Hotel every Saturday night, and I'd bring Ron along. Detachable mink collars were in style then. Ron would take my collar and put it on his head to make everyone at our table laugh.

Despite working full time and raising Ron, I managed to get out and have fun. The cost of a babysitter for a Saturday night was part of the reason I'd take Ronnie with me. Then a friend of mine, who had a hard time getting together with her boyfriend, volunteered to be my babysitter. I knew he visited her at my place but she babysat for free, so it was fine with me.

Twice I tried to marry rich men. Everything about each one was fine except that I couldn't stand the idea of sleeping with the guy. One of them was real nice. I introduced him to someone I knew, and he married her.

My dating life changed forever one snowy Valentine's Day. It was so stormy I almost didn't go out that evening, but I had promised to pick up a nursing school classmate who put up with me despite all my crazy doings, so I drove my trusty Crosley through the falling snow. We arrived at the Hazel Park Commercial Club on White Bear Avenue and started dancing. The club manager phoned his brother Joe to come over because "There's a blonde here who wants to dance with you." I love to dance and both brothers were excellent dancers. But Joe was really good and we danced the night away. We did dance beautifully together. Turns out Joe had been an instructor at the Arthur Murray Dance Studio in New York. He also had a taxi business when he lived there. He, his two brothers, and their mother had come from Switzerland to settle in the U.S. His mother lived in North Dakota with other relatives.

The next evening Joe showed up at my apartment even though I had another date. I didn't recall telling him where I lived. "Do you mind if I babysit Ron?" he asked. "Us guys have a lot in common." So he'd take care of Ron and I'd go out on dates. By this time, Ron and I were living in the duplex on George Street, and Katie, our live-in caretaker who had been with us for over two years, stayed with us during the week. Joe would drop by even when I wasn't home. He'd tell Katie he was stopping in to say hi to Ron. He saw more of Ron than he did of me. Of course, Ron would do his "You go be my daddy?" routine on Joe like I taught him. Joe and I did go out on dates and always had a wonderful time dancing. It was a crazy courtship.

I had gotten a legal separation from Bud when I returned to St. Paul after living with my parents in North Dakota for Ron's first year, but I didn't give him a divorce. I declared that he had deserted me and the baby. When Joe and I started getting serious, I went ahead and filed for a divorce. Six months after getting the divorce, Joe and I married in September of 1955.

The morning of our wedding, Joe came over to the West Side duplex on George Street. When Ron saw we were leaving, he asked, "Can't I go with you?" Katie said, "They are going away to get married. You will have a real daddy when they come back."

Katie and Ronnie waved us off. We drove south to Northwood, Iowa, where we were married by a Justice of the Peace. The people in his office were our witnesses. We drove to Albert Lea in Minnesota, stayed overnight in a hotel and came back the next day. A cheap wedding. I didn't want a big wedding. I've had two cheap weddings. I was working for the government when I married Bud during the war and we got married by a Justice of the Peace in a nearby town. I've always had the feeling that women who have to have the perfect wedding do so to satisfy something within themselves. They want to be the special center of everything for at least one big day. I'm always the center of attention, so I didn't need to do that!

After we returned, my friends gave us a party at the Hazel Park Commercial Club where Joe's brother was still the manager. The folks at

3M arranged for a five-piece band. The party—cake and everything—was all furnished by my friends. I was amazed that so many people came to wish us well.

Bud remarried two months after I married Joe. He had come back to the Twin Cities then moved with his new wife to California where they had a son who is about the same age as my second son, Mark. I still see his sister and play golf with his niece. I kept in touch with all the family. When Bud's mother went into a nursing home, Ron would go out to see her. When she died, I went to her funeral. Bud eventually died in California of an aneurism. Even though he was Ron's biological father, they never knew each other.

What goes around comes around. With all that had happened, I never once said a derogatory thing to Ron about his biological father. He'd refer to Bud as his real father and to Joe as his dad. Ron was eight years old when he got a full-time dad. Joe was good to Ron. He was a fine father to him. He didn't interfere with how I raised Ron and mostly kept his opinions to himself even after we married. He always treated and loved Ron the same as his own kids.

When Joe came from Switzerland to New York where he had relatives, he married and had a son named after him who died in infancy. Then they had a daughter Joan and two sons, Jay and Paul. Joe and his kids moved to St. Paul to be near relatives. His wife came out but didn't like the Midwest. She went back East while he stayed here with his kids. When Joe and I decided to marry, he went ahead with his divorce. Paul was a few years older than Ron. He stayed with us for a year then moved to New York to live with his mother. Jay remained in St Paul, but eventually moved back East with his wife and kids. Joan wasn't too happy with me at the beginning of our relationship. I don't blame her. She and her husband had just gotten married and were living with Joe when Ron and I appeared on the scene. Eventually we worked it out. Joe was always a kind, generous person. He had lots of love to go around.

Joe worked at a nearby company, but I encouraged him to apply to 3M, so he got a job there in maintenance and repair. I usually worked the 7:00 A.M. to 3:30 P.M. shift, and he worked 3:00 to 11:00 P.M. Despite work and family pressures, life was good, and we were happy.

Joe was definitely a jack-of-all-trades and the master of quite a few. It was his skills that enabled us to take on the huge job of remodeling the old farmhouse that Joe was renting on McKnight Road near 3M when we met. After our wedding, Ron and I moved in with Joe. The two-story farmhouse needed lots of work. It had awful wallpaper, and the floors and windows had to be replaced, but Joe was able to fix it up. We had a large yard with space to plant flowers, vegetables, and fruit trees.

Before long we decided to buy the house. Between the two of us, we came up with the down payment of four thousand dollars for the house and the land. Gradually we brought the old four-bedroom farmhouse up to code and eventually added on to it. The south wall of the kitchen had to be rebuilt. It took us a good year to get it under control. The new kitchen wallpaper I picked out had scenes exactly like the farm I was raised on in North Dakota with black and white Holstein cows, pigs, chickens and roosters, a red barn, and a cream-colored house.

One Saturday I came home after running an errand. Joe was hanging the wallpaper in the kitchen. He was wearing glasses. I had never seen him wear glasses before. He turned around and when he saw me, he said, "Oh, my God, I never knew what you looked like."

"It's a little late now, don't you think?"

ఠ 15 ଔ

Making a New Family

J oe wanted more children, and I did too. I was really happy to find I was pregnant, even though it meant I would have to leave my job at 3M. I had a plan, though. Several plans. The first one was to have the baby by cesarean—an absolute necessity given my small size. Since I could choose the date, I planned the baby's birth for October 31. I'd have a Halloween baby and always have a big party to celebrate!

The first scare associated with the baby's Halloween birth happened on the way to the hospital the night before. Ron, who was ten at the time, was in the back seat. The plan was to pick up Joe after his night shift, then he and Ron were to take me to the hospital. I must have been thinking about giving birth again after ten years because Ron called out suddenly, "Mom, Mom! You drove right by Daddy. He's standing back there on the corner."

When we finally got to the hospital and they dropped me off, I visited with all the medical staff I knew on the night shift. Then I went to my room to prepare for surgery at six in the morning. With a cesarean birth, I would avoid trauma for the baby. The delivery went fine except that I had the strangest experience with the anesthesia. I was put under completely or so they told me. But I wasn't unconscious. Instead, I had visions, visual effects, and one adventure after the other. Not tranquil at all. I saw swarms of red, lots of color—like psychedelic scenes. It was spooky and a bit scary. I felt I was being subjected to a movie I hadn't intended to see. Later I talked to the anesthesiologist and asked him what they had given me. He said curare was in the anesthesia. That's what the Indians in Brazil used to coat their poisonous arrowheads to kill people.

Back in the fifties men weren't usually present at the birth of their children. They hung out in the waiting room. That's where Joe was when Mark was born October 31, 1956. My mother came from North Dakota to be with us for a month and help me out. Ron was very happy to have a baby brother. He held little Mark in his arms and talked to him. Mark was a cute baby. We called him our Matzo ball baby because he was round and firmly packed. With his reddish gold curls and turquoise-colored eyes, Mark looked like a Gerber Foods ad. I bought him a turquoise parka with white fur. People commented, "What a pretty little girl!" I'd say "Thank you!"

"That's not right," my mother exclaimed. "You should correct them."

"I'm not going to explain," I answered. "If they think he's a girl, so what!"

Mark has a strong memory and even remembers me bathing him in the sink. But he never mentioned being mistaken for a girl, so I don't think it affected him.

I worked at my 3M nursing job until two weeks before Mark was born. In the 1950s women couldn't go back to work after childbirth. Once you had a pregnancy, you were out of the workforce. For the most part, that didn't change until the women's movement in the 1970s, but 3M modified their rule a few years after I left. However, I was able to start working again when Mark was six weeks old. I belonged to the Minnesota Fourth District Nurses Association and had put my name in to be called as a private duty nurse. The association placed nurses with patients. As it turned out, I got most of my work by recommendation and word of mouth. I worked for a lot of people on Summit Avenue, the street in St. Paul with big mansions owned by wealthy families. I had great flexibility. I could set my pay and create a schedule that let me take care of my own family. Joe worked nights and stayed home during the day. I think he was a better mother than I was. I can remember little Mark hanging on to his dad's pant leg. He'd look up at him appreciatively and say, "You're a good mommy, Daddy."

Among the things Joe would do with Mark was take him along bowling. Joe loved to bowl. He'd sit Mark in a highchair right in front of the lanes. Mark got a dime for every strike.

Joe became a first-time grandfather the same year Mark was born. His daughter Joan—I called her Joanniebell—and her husband had a girl, Joanne, in March. They had two more girls, one two years later and the last girl, ten years later. Joe's son Jay and his wife raised their four children here, so Joe had lots of kids and grandkids around.

Even though I had to juggle my time off around the needs and schedules of my patients, I made sure we took family vacations. One summer we rented a cabin on Strawberry Lake in Minnesota where the parents of a friend of mine owned a resort. Mark was still a baby and Ron was about twelve. We went out fishing in a rowboat. Joe was rowing. I had Mark with me. Ron was in the back of the boat with a fishing line. He kept saying "Look! Look!" But we didn't pay any attention, as usual. Finally we checked his line and he had the largest Northern Pike we ever saw tagging along behind the boat. Ron was so excited. We had to row back to shore and get my father to help us bring in that fish. Joe and I wrestled with it. I held Mark in one arm and helped Joe with the other. I was worried we'd tip the boat over. We told Ron that he was the best fisherman. Ron's catch impressed everyone at the resort, and that night we had a good fish dinner.

I wanted Ron to have normal childhood experiences like other kids, so I started a Cub Scout troop with my neighbor Leona who lived across the street. Her kids were about the same age as Ron. We met in my basement. We had eight young boys in the troop. Our best project was with bottle caps. The kids nailed them upside down to a square of wood to make a mud scraper for dirty shoes.

At that time I had plenty of yarn and knitting needles on hand, so I decided to teach the boys how to knit. They learned, but probably had more fun brandishing the needles like swords when I wasn't looking. Strange but true, I ran into one of the boys many years later.

"How do you like my sweater?" he asked me.

"It's beautiful," I said.

"I still knit and I made it," he told me.

I think he was the only one who kept on knitting.

Another project involved taking wire coat hangers and straightening them out to make marshmallow roasters. The kids then painted the handles which were made of empty wooden thread spools. I had set up the whole project outdoors. Little Mark was there with the boys even though he was only three. I gave him a container of water and a brush. Somehow Mark managed to get into the paint of the boy next to him and painted half his curly, fiery red hair green. We had a dentist appointment right after the Scout meeting so I had no time to clean him up. I took him to the dentist just as he was. I pretended that he was supposed to look that way.

"Where did you get the leprechaun?" the dentist asked.

Joe was born and raised in Switzerland, so it was a logical choice to name our girl Heidi. I wanted her to be born on Valentine's Day, also by cesarean, but she didn't keep her end of the deal. She came early.

Heidi Jo Ann was born early in the morning on February 3, 1960, by C-section. It was different having such a small baby. She weighed just six pounds. Heidi was born four years after Mark. I had told Mark that he would have someone to play with when the new baby came. I called him several times from the hospital to tell him about his little sister. He was very excited to think he'd have a playmate.

On a cold, windy, snowy day I brought Heidi home all bundled up. I unwrapped her and held her up to Ron and Mark.

"Now we have a real family," said Ron. I felt that way myself because for so long there had just been the two of us. We had been pretty much alone. All of my extended family was older, and they weren't able to be around much or to help. My parents were the youngest in both their families.

Mark, however, just stared at Heidi. Disappointment showed on his face. "Mom, please take her back."

"But, Mark, she'll grow. You'll see. You'll be able to play together." He just looked at me totally disillusioned. Whenever Joe asked Mark, "Don't you want to kiss your little sister?" he'd say, "No." Ron, though, loved Heidi.

Joe's Aunt Ida came to live with us for a while and help out with the baby. She loved to cook. Happy day! Aunt Ida was quite a plump person, and Heidi loved nestling in her arms. She didn't cuddle up with me because I was too bony.

Mark persisted in not caring for Heidi. On a warm spring day, Mark was playing in the house and Heidi was in a bassinet that I moved from room to room. I was working in the kitchen. I peeked in the bassinet to check on the baby, but she was gone. The door to the outside was open and I feared the worst—that someone had come in and taken the baby. Then I heard whimpering. I looked around and found her under the sofa. Mark had taken Heidi out of her bassinet and tucked her under the couch. I was not happy with Mark. I sent him to bed immediately. I kept an eye on him after that. When they were both outside together and I was in the house I'd say, "Mark, watch out for the baby."

"It's not my baby," he'd call back. It took him a long time to warm up to his little sister.

It must have been around this age that Mark crawled up a huge tree and perched way out on a limb. My neighbor Leona called me on the phone. "Mark is hanging from a tree," she said. I looked out and saw him. I called her back. "Don't say anything to him. I'll just watch. If I say anything, he could fall." She stood in her doorway giving me a progress report as he inched his way back to the main trunk then down to the ground.

I always told Mark not to forget his "pleases" and "thank yous." I guess he remembered. The same neighbor had a party for the children. Leona later told me, "Your son came up to me when the party was over. He said, 'Mrs. Farrell, thank you for a very nice party.' He was the only child who ever thanked me for the party. I couldn't get over it. He knew who did all the work."

We had a storage space on the top floor of our remodeled farmhouse. That's where I kept my old clothes that I hoped would come back into style some day. Whenever I wanted to get something, I sent Mark up there because he was light enough not to break through the attic floor and come through the ceiling. I always wondered if his ventures into the dark, cramped attic space sparked his later interest in exploring caves.

Easter was a major celebration at our house. We'd go to church dressed in our new Easter finery. Then we'd have a big meal with family. We also had Easter baskets for the kids. "This is what the Easter Bunny left you," we told them. But when Mark was about four or five, he woke up and came downstairs and saw Joe and me putting candy in the baskets. That finished the Easter Bunny for him. Joe really enjoyed hiding Easter eggs for the kids, though. He enjoyed it so much that he hid eggs each Easter until he died. The "kids" had to hunt for the eggs even when they had their own children!

As our children grew, so did their relationships with each other. Ron was the older brother—a special one who was not only much older but who often needed extra care because he was experiencing the effects of cerebral palsy or recuperating from surgery. Ron participated when he could, but his life was on its own track running parallel to theirs. Mark and Heidi, though, were always attentive and helpful toward Ron.

Heidi's attitude toward her other big brother was the opposite of Mark's early feelings towards her. Heidi hung around Mark so much and followed him wherever he went in the neighborhood that his buddies called her "Shadow." "Here comes Mark's Shadow," they'd say.

Every summer my mother went on vacation with us. She was our built-in babysitter. We rented two cabins. She stayed in one with the kids, while Joe and I were in another. Mother could get away from the kids when we took them with us. Sometimes we rented a trailer to go camping, but my mother wasn't much of a camper. Whenever she was away from home, she would leave her cat with the neighbors back in North Dakota. They always knew when she was coming back home, because the cat would begin a ritual of walking over to her house daily until she returned. My parents continued being a great support to us. Even as they aged, they would come to St. Paul by train to visit.

Despite both of us working, Joe and I didn't bring in a lot of money. But I was used to scrimping and making do. I've been poor but never in debt. No matter what, I never got myself into debt.

Our Christmas treat when the kids were young was to go downtown and look at the store windows all decorated for the holidays. We'd go to Woolworth's and sit at the counter to have lunch and a soda after seeing the windows. Of course, the kids would say, "I want this. I want that. I'm going to ask Santa for it." But I'd tell them, "Oh, that's pretty expensive. I don't think Santa Claus has that much money."

When there's no money, there's nothing for extras like loads of toys. But I feel kids play best with pans and cardboard boxes anyway. I had latches on the kitchen cupboard doors. Once in a while I'd open them up and let the kids play with all the pots and pans. My kids had everything they needed but nothing extra. I think it's a good way to raise kids. It taught them valuable lessons.

I feel sorry for those kids now whose folks give them everything because then children expect everything. But I always gave my kids love and attention no matter how busy I was. Those early years go by too fast.

๑ 16 ๏

Making an Impression on Your Kids

When things got too dull and quiet around me, I would do something to make life interesting. But once I had kids, I no longer had to worry about livening things up. They did it all. They created enough activity and problems for me. By the time I worked eight hours a day, cooked, cleaned the house, looked after my parents, checked on the kids, helped Ron and made sure he was okay, entertained at home with Joe or went out dancing with him, I didn't really need to create too much more to keep me busy. In all these goings on, however, I always had to be inventive and resourceful—one way or the other.

We had a small boat on a trailer. Often in the summer I'd take the kids to a nearby lake. Joe would be at work. Well, despite learning to drive a truck at a young age, guiding monster farm equipment and surviving many car challenges, I could never back the boat trailer down to the dock straight. So I'd purposely place it at such an awkward angle that some nice man would come over and help me back it down and put the boat into the water for us.

Heidi and Mark were so different. Heidi was always zinging with high energy. There was no quietness about her. She'd be friends one day, enemies the next. With Mark, however, you never knew what he was thinking. He never had enemies and never got into fights. I had a conference with his fifth grade teacher, Mr. Johnson. "I've never had a student like him," he told me. "He doesn't look at me when I'm lecturing. Instead he's watching a squirrel in the tree. He's not there in the classroom with us." This worried me. Mark didn't seem interested in school. He complained that no one wanted him on their team for spelling bees. I wondered if he had a hearing problem but he tested out fine. I even used flash cards with him to help him get better grades. Then he had a teacher in seventh grade who took an interest in him and realized Mark was just bored by school. He had been reading easy books. No one challenged him. Mark switched to advanced classes, started paying attention and ended up one of the top students in the school.

Our backyard was all the former open farmland around us. Part of it used to be a plum orchard. We picked blackberries there. I usually put in a vegetable garden on land close to the house. Way back was an area with trees that the kids called the Witch's Woods. It broke out into a knoll with grasses. The kids skied on it in winter. I felt as if we were living in heaven on earth. Neighborhood kids came to fly kites and hang out there. One day, someone—probably Mark—was playing with matches and the field caught fire. The whole neighborhood showed up to help put it out.

The backyard was the perfect setting for the Halloween parties held on Mark's birthday. We'd build a big bonfire. Each year the trees grew and closed in more. One year the bonfire reached up so high that the leaves caught fire. We put that fire out with a garden hose.

Mark's Halloween birthday party included spooky stories told around the bonfire. To give the kids a scare, a neighbor snuck up into the tree near the bonfire wearing a sheet. People five houses away reported hearing the kids' shrieks.

Probably because the area used to be farmland, people dropped off the cats they didn't want. Periodically an abandoned kitten or cat would appear on our doorstep, so we always had a cat around the house. Unlike my mother, I am not particularly fond of cats and Mark isn't either. Heidi, though, loves cats and all animals. She was forever bringing in stray animals and taking care of them. One of our cats had the habit of crawling up onto the damper in the fireplace to sleep. We found this out when Joe lit a fire and suddenly the cat leapt from the fireplace and flew out the door as the kids were coming in. The cat was singed and smoking, but it survived.

Once Heidi rescued a baby robin that had fallen from its nest. She put the robin in a cage and fed it. The little bird grew feathers, but unfortunately didn't survive long enough to go back to the wild. On another occasion, Heidi found a lost puppy in the neighborhood, brought it home and cared for it until she figured out who it belonged to and returned it to the happy owners.

A huge wild turkey limped into the yard one day. He must have known we were friendly because he stayed for several weeks. We fed him. He flew around and got to be a regular in the neighborhood before he left.

We also had bats in the attic. Mark convinced the neighbors that they were his pet bats that he let out of their cages at night. The neighbors saw the bats come out and believed him. They remarked to other neighbors and friends about the boy with the pet bats! They were more than a little embarrassed when they got wise to Mark's joke.

Mark always seemed to know exactly what he wanted and how to go after it. At age twelve he worked all summer on his cousin's farm cleaning chicken coops and riding horses. He made a hundred and fifty dollars and bought his first motorcycle, a used one. He took classes on how to ride and care for it. When he was thirteen, he got a job at the local liquor store hauling bottles. He worked there lugging beer bottles for five years. He did well in high school and was a member of the honor society. I got a call from one of his teachers asking why Mark, Joe, and I hadn't attended the honor society banquet. Mark never said anything because he was working that night. When I asked why he didn't tell us about the banquet, he replied that work was more important.

The owners of the liquor store, Carmen and Gus, were good friends of ours. That's how Mark had gotten the job. One day he was in the back room sorting bottles. Through an opening, he saw a customer stashing a bottle under his jacket. Mark went over to Gus and pointed the guy out. When he came to the cash register and paid for his purchase, Gus asked him, "Is that all?"

"What do you mean?"

"What about that bottle under your jacket?" The guy was mad but turned over the stolen bottle.

Gus was pleased. "This kid's on the ball," he said and raised Mark's wages. When Mark turned eighteen, he began making deliveries for them.

At the time that Heidi started school, the trend in classrooms was shifting from rows of desks in straight lines to an open format with tables arranged in groups and space for the kids to sit on the floor. Heidi's third grade teacher created an open room, and Heidi brought in her own chenille rug for all the kids to sit on. I often volunteered to be the nurse at the kids' schools. That way I could check in on them and see how they were doing.

Mark and Heidi noticed that when the neighbor kids got sick, they would go to the doctor. "How come you never take us to the doctor?" they complained. I told them, "You don't need to go to the doctor. You've got me." Besides using my nursing skills, I would recite "magic words" to the kids when bandaging their cuts or curing their colds.

Nurses are definite people. We tend to see things black or white, yes or no without fuzzy gray areas. We are used to taking charge, assuming responsibility for situations and making quick decisions. The kids could twist their dad around their fingers, but not me. Joe would tell them, "You just wait till your mother gets home." When Heidi would protest and complain, I would remind her, "There's no law that says you have to love your mother, but you'd better obey me."

When the kids used bad words or lied, I'd wash their mouths out with soap. I had a special sweet glycerin rose soap. They knew they'd get a mouthful of suds if they used bad language. Whatever negative behavior they showed, I firmly nipped it in the bud.

When Mark was about twelve, he built a tree house in a big tree out back. He had Heidi working for him. She hauled pieces of wood like his slave. She would make things for him and bring him snacks. Then when he was finished, he put up a big sign that said, "No girls allowed." Oh, was she mad.

One night Mark and his buddy David—the two are still friends—were going to camp outside in the backyard tree house. We had it all arranged. David's parents knew he would be safe in the yard after curfew. Kids under sixteen weren't supposed to be out alone on the streets after midnight. I had never had a problem with Mark or his friend. So we all went to bed. Well, about two in the morning we got a call from the police station. The kids had been picked up for violating curfew.

I arrived at the Maplewood police station along with David's father. The police station had just been redone. "My, this is a lovely place," I said. "Very comfortable. Maybe we should leave the kids here. At least they'd be safe and we'd know where they are." The guy at the desk and David's dad nearly fell over. We did take the boys home, but later Mark asked me, "Mom, would you really have left me there?" "Of course," I told him. "It was such a nice place and we would have known exactly where you were."

Only much later did I find out that Mark and David regularly walked over to the nearby drive-in theater to watch movies. One of them would sneak in and turn the speakers up loud, then they'd both sit outside the fence and watch the movie. That night they had been picked up walking home from their night at the movies.

I also learned that Mark and his buddies used to hop trains and ride them back and forth to the different switch houses. On their sojourns, they got to know hobos and visited hobo camps. They flattened coins and strips of copper on the tracks and who knows what else they did! I'm glad I didn't know about this when they were doing it. I had enough to think about.

When Heidi entered puberty, she began getting the idea she could do as she wanted. I worked evenings, and she was supposed to be at home. Ron was home and knew that Heidi was expected to be home too. One night he called me and said that Heidi hadn't come back yet. I checked around to see if there had been an accident. Then I got Mark. "Mark, we have to find your sister. We're going to the police station." That's where we found her. She was with some boys that the police picked up for having an open can of beer in the car.

"Well, since I can't trust this girl," I said to myself, "I'll just have to keep her close by me." So every evening for two weeks Heidi came with me to work. I was doing private duty nursing for a patient of mine who was at Miller Hospital. I had the evening shift. Heidi would sit in the lobby doing her homework. I packed a brown bag supper for her and that's what she ate while I had a nice hot meal in the cafeteria. "Why isn't your daughter eating with us?" the other nurses asked me. "She has her food. She's fine," I assured them. I never had any problem with Heidi after that.

The kids had their chores to do around the house and yard, especially in the summertime. That was another tactic to keep them busy. I'm sure they were more interested in hanging out and enjoying summer activities, but that's how I ran things. When Joe's son Paul came to visit over the summer from New York, he also got a list of tasks that included cutting the huge lawn with our push mower. He borrowed three lawn mowers from neighbors and recruited some kids to help him do the job fast. I fear my list of chores eventually dampened his enthusiasm for coming to visit his dad and half-siblings. I even gave tasks to Mark and Heidi's friends who showed up at the house.

Mark sang with the Tartan Choir from his high school. In 1974 the choir went to Europe to sing Christmas morning at the Cathedral of Notre Dame. They even made a recording. As part of their trip, each choir member had to bring something identifiably from the United States to give their hosts. Mark brought popcorn.

The night they were to leave on their trip, I drove Mark and his friend to the airport. The instruments and piano got loaded into the belly of the plane they were taking to Europe, but it started to snow so heavily that the plane couldn't leave. The kids had to return home. I had Heidi and Ron with me in my white Monte Carlo. We drove under a bridge just as a snowplow was passing by overhead. It dumped so much snow onto the car that we couldn't move. Then we got hit from behind by another car. What a mess! Mark and his buddy had to scrape the snow away by hand. Finally we managed to get free and make it home. Of course, I had to drive them back to the airport at 6:00 A.M. the next morning.

When Mark started college, he bought himself an old jeep. He'd drive Ron, who was still living at home with us, to his job. Mark attended Lakewood Community College for two years and then enrolled at the University of Minnesota in mechanical engineering with a minor in solar engineering. He also started working part time at the local utilities company, Northern States Power (now Xcel Energy), to pay for his education.

At some point during his college career, the Navy tried to recruit Mark and a friend. Mark wasn't interested. I thought he was missing a good opportunity. "Here's your chance to be on a sub," I told him.

"I don't want to be on a submarine," he informed me. I practically had to chloroform him to get him to go to the interview. "Mom, it's dishonest to go if I know I'm not interested," he told me.

"Just go and check it out." I said. "You'll get a free meal." Not only did he get a free meal, they flew him out to the coast to visit a Trident submarine and meet the crew.

They assured him the food was tops. "You'll never forget how good this clam chowder is," they bragged at the dinner for the potential recruits. "It's made with cream sherry." He liked the clam chowder, but it didn't convince Mark to enlist in the Navy, especially after he saw the minuscule rooms that slept four. It was way too claustrophobic for him. I could sympathize. I can't stand being confined to small spaces.

Tornadoes are a reality of late spring and summer in Minnesota. When the wailing sirens pierce the air, everyone is supposed to head to the basement. Perhaps because I don't like to be confined, I'd throw a party whenever tornado warnings sounded. Everyone loved it when the sirens went off. All the neighbors would come to my basement. I'd bring out food and drinks and we'd party. We usually kept on partying well after the danger was over. It served as a distraction for us, and I didn't mind having to hunker down in the basement. We looked forward to tornado season!

ഇ 17 ൙

The Rarefied World of Private Duty Nursing

I got to know a number of rich and sometimes famous people in my life but usually over thermometers and blood pressure cuffs. I worked as a private duty nurse with many of the old wealthy families of the Twin Cities. Their names are familiar because of the streets and places named after them. Work came through recommendations and word of mouth. My assignments often lasted several years. I truly enjoyed private duty nursing. It was an education and a chance to know and work with many notable people. I always marveled that I was able to use nursing to make my life so interesting and to bring happiness and comfort to others. At least that's what they told me.

One gentleman I worked for was a banker who had a heart condition. My work day started with a ride to his downtown office with him in his limousine. I'd check his pulse and heart rate a few times over the four hours I attended him. When I wasn't doing that, I'd sit in the office reception area and knit or read.

I worked for Mrs. McKnight (the family that founded 3M) on the 7:00 A.M. to 3:00 P.M. shift for over five years. We would do things together, and she often organized trips and outings. Once we had a picnic at a park overlooking the St. Croix River in Stillwater. We arrived in the limo. Mrs. McKnight and I visited while Celso, the Filipino driver, pulled a card table and folding chairs out of the limo and set them up. He spread an embroidered linen tablecloth on the table and put out napkins and fingerbowls with flowers floating in them. He set the table with silverware, china, crystal goblets, candles, and a bouquet of flowers. We started out with double daiquiris. Mrs. McKnight said it was a special occasion that merited double daiquiris. She always insisted I have a daiquiri with her. Then Celso, dressed in a white jacket, served us the elegant gourmet meal the cook had prepared and sent along.

I always wore my white cap and uniform when I worked for Mrs. McKnight. When she rode in her car, she sat on a pivot seat so she could swing out easily. I'd get out on the other side. Celso, in his full uniform, would bring around a collapsible wheelchair. We'd get out in front of the Lowry Medical Building downtown and go in the back door. She never had to wait to be seen by the doctor.

Some of the people I cared for spent the winter at their estates in Florida, so they paid me a retainer until they returned to Minnesota in the spring. I would fly down with them on their personal planes. One client had a gated island complete with a yacht. They would show me around for a few days before flying me back home.

My husband Joe used to tell me, "For all the fun you have, you shouldn't get paid."

I worked nights at the Griggs mansion, one of the large, old mansions on Summit Avenue. A distinguishing feature of the house was the large wooden, wheel-like chandelier in the central hallway. The chandelier was decorated with carved mice. Mrs. Griggs liked mice. Trust me, they were truly realistic.

One of the rooms in the mansion was her dead husband's study. During the night shift, I swear I could hear movement in there. Mrs.

Griggs had told me that her late husband always came back at night to work in his study. I'd sit by the fireplace in my little room wondering what I would say to him if he opened the door and walked in.

I told Joe about this. "You're crazy," he said.

"I know that," I told him. Still, you get involved and begin to wonder—is it me or what? The longtime employees there told me the same thing.

Mrs. Griggs's daughter, who was older than I was, came back from China with all sorts of beautiful silks that she showed me one day. While we were visiting, I asked her if the ghost of her father was in the house. She said, "Oh yes. I believe it."

When Mrs. Griggs made a thousand-dollar donation to Dwight Eisenhower's presidential campaign, she received an "Ike for President" gold pin which she then gave to me and I still have.

I also took care of Mrs. O'Shaughnessy. Mr. and Mrs. O'Shaughnessy had only two employees—Irene to cook and clean and Frank who helped with the house and driving. The O'Shaughnessys didn't waste money. Irene told me that Mr. O'Shaughnessy had formal clothes but that he had only three shirts to use for business, so she constantly had to wash them. A Saudi Arabian king sent them 24-carat solid gold service plates to eat on. When Irene opened them, she asked what they were going to do with them. Mr. O'Shaughnessy replied, "Just tie them up again and put them under the cabinet."

Mrs. O'Shaughnessy showed me around the house when I first came to work there. "Remember," she said, "we use our bath towels three times before washing them." I had to shake them out and hang them up to dry whenever I used them.

When my family comes to stay with me, they toss their towels into the wash after one use. When I visit my daughter, she tells me to throw the towels on the floor after using them once and she'll wash them. "We only use clean, fresh towels, Mom."

"Well," I point out, "the rich people I work for—the millionaires—they reused their bath towels."

When I was still a young nurse and long before the World War II started, I was back in St. Paul. A doctor I knew asked if I would be interested in going to Los Angeles with a widowed heiress. She was staying at the St. Paul Hotel. She was an alcoholic. The hotel had called the doctor for her. Now she wanted to go back to LA and needed someone to travel with her. I said sure. The next day we had a double compartment on the train to LA. I never thought that I would remain with her for seventeen months. She was a Hershey chocolate heiress. I lived in my own room at the house in LA. I was on twenty-four-hour duty. She liked to talk except when she clipped food coupons from the newspaper every morning. I didn't bother her when she was clipping her coupons. Between the chauffeur and me, we had to make sure she didn't drink. My duties were to entertain her, go out shopping, and go out for drives. When she had people over, I had to keep an eye on her. Her husband had been an executive at Paramount and she still owned stock in Paramount studios, so we often went to studio parties. I met Pat O'Brien, Joan Crawford, and many others. I could wear her dresses, especially party dresses cut on the bias. She also let me use the phone to call long distance and talk to my family in North Dakota.

In order to look great for all these parties, I decided to work on a tan. I slathered on all sorts of oils and took time from my busy schedule of caring for the heiress to sit in the sun in the vast yard. Then I'd come in and show my arms to Lavoncel, the main cook, who was African-American. "You're not so dark, child," she said, putting her arm next to mine.

The heiress had a twenty-year-old son. I was twenty-seven. As part of my duties, I had to see that he did not get out of line because he was set to marry a Denver heiress, and his mother didn't want him to be contaminated by getting involved with anyone else. So two mornings a week, the chauffer took us to Griffin Park, and we rode horses there together. When he went out to parties in the evenings with his friends, I'd go as his girlfriend. Sometimes we'd go on boat parties. It was a life I had never experienced. I didn't spend any money. I was able to save up a lot and not work for a while after that.

I also took care of a member of the family whose Summit Avenue house is now the governor's mansion. It belonged to a former governor, H.H. Irvine. My patient was Clotilde, or Cloti as she was called, the former governor's granddaughter. She was a lovely person and someone I got close to as she was dying. I was with her for over two years.

Their property was at White Bear Lake, an area on the edge of St. Paul favored by the wealthy. F. Scott Fitzgerald, author of *The Great Gatsby*, described life there in his early writings.

When Clotilde died, I received an engraved invitation to her funeral which was held at the White Bear estate. It was a beautiful, sunny afternoon. The funeral was at 2:00 P.M. As I drove over the bridge that spanned a moat around the property, Clotilde was suddenly seated beside me in my car. She was wearing a pink, sequined dress that she loved. She often wore that dress. I wasn't afraid. I turned to her and said, "I'm so glad to see you." She had a low, lilting voice and said, "Thank you." On the other side of the moat she was gone. I arrived at the funeral. The ceremony was going to take place outside. Her sister asked me if I would like to come in and see Clotilde in her casket. "No," I said. "I'll remember her as I saw her coming over the bridge," and I explained that I had seen her.

"What was she wearing?" her sister asked.

"That beautiful pink dress she loved so much," I told her.

"That's the dress she's buried in."

18

Moving on with Ron

When I married Joe and we moved into the house in the St. Paul suburb of Maplewood, I decided to send Ron to first grade at the nearby public elementary school, Beaver Lake. I felt that contact with other children was worth more than having him do school work at his grade level. This was also the recommendation of a psychologist who had seen him. Ron's comprehension and ability to sort out things was greater than most kids his age.

So in 1955 at the age of eight, Ron went off to school like other kids. He walked but he wasn't too stable on his feet. That meant kids could push him down on purpose or he'd get jostled and fall. When he came home, he would tell me about these incidents, and then say, "But I'm going back tomorrow." He seemed to take it as a part of life. Ron was the only disabled child at the school for the first few years.

Shortly after he started school, he came home one day beaming and announced, "Guess what, Mom? I have a friend."

"That's wonderful, Ron. Who's that?"

"His name is Dwight, and he lives near here. Know what, Mom?"

"What?"

"He doesn't have anything wrong with him. And he's going to be my friend."

Ron seemed to think it was so great to have a friend who didn't have a disability. That was one time his disability really hit me. He faced it every day, every minute. I never remember him complaining, though. My other two kids complained about everything, but Ron didn't. He'd get frustrated and upset but he never sassed me or complained—even the day he decided to walk in the mud like the other kids. He got stuck and fell down. I had to help him up. "It looked like fun, Mom," he said as I cleaned the mud off.

He played baseball, though. Ron always wore his cap to school. I asked him why. "That's how I play baseball. I catch the ball with my cap. And you know, the other kids try but they can't catch it like I do."

I usually volunteered as a school nurse and helped with shots and other medical matters. I was able to keep in close contact with Ron's teachers that way.

Cerebral palsy is not a static condition. Nerves, muscles, and the brain are all interrelated and affected by growth, use, atrophy from lack of use, and various treatments including therapy and surgery. Thus Ron's physical appearance and abilities changed over time. As he grew older, he didn't have that much control of his face, and he developed facial grimaces, especially when he was under stress. One eye opened more than the other. His mouth was twisted, and his head was cocked to one side. He drooled because of lack of control over facial and head muscles. For the most part, I was the only one who could understand his speech. This made his presentation to others, especially to kids, difficult. It wasn't easy for him to fit in, but I wasn't aware of how hard it was for him because he never complained.

All this time, we kept up Ron's exercises. He was making steady but very gradual progress. Even though Ron kept receiving therapy under the supervision of therapists at Gillette Children's Hospital, I continued to look for ways to help Ron.

I really tried everything for Ron. I even found a Chinese doctor who did acupuncture. This was long before people here knew much about Chinese medicine and before acupuncture was licensed. Ron had daily treatments for several months. I tried it too. We noticed that the treatments improved his spasticity, leg control, and speech. Of course, the regular doctors thought this was crazy, so I told Ron not to mention the treatments when we visited his doctor.

As Ron grew older, he had a series of operations to lengthen his heel tendons. This is pretty much standard procedure for those with cerebral palsy. The operations enabled him to walk and counteracted the contraction of his leg tendons. His surgeries were performed at the University of Minnesota by Dr. Essam Awad, a longtime member of the Department of Physical Medicine and Rehabilitation. Ron thought the surgeon was a magician. During one of Ron's stays at the hospital, his roommate was a university football player who had been thrown from a motorcycle. They became friends and even kept in touch after they left the hospital. I drove to the university so often that I could make the trip with my eyes shut.

When you're in charge of someone, especially someone with a disability, you tend to make decisions without consulting the other person. At least, that's what I did. Looking back over the years I can see that many of the decisions I made for him were, in fact, one-sided. I thought, "This is what he should do." But not very often did I ask him, "Is this what you want?" I was too busy planning how things should be. In dealing with young adults with physical or other problems, it's all too easy to neglect getting their input.

My excuse was that I was working all the time and felt I needed everything lined up and well organized. I soothed my inner soul by believing I was doing the very best I could, but now I recognize that I didn't take into consideration a lot of smaller things along the way. When I took Ron out of Lindsay School and mainstreamed him, I was aware that I was putting him in with people who probably wouldn't make the effort to understand and accommodate him. I knew there would be problems, but I was busy planning when I probably should have taken several deep breaths and calmly considered the entire situation. Hindsight is always twenty-twenty, but this has been a big lesson for me.

People who are responsible for others—I include myself—think they have to guide the person they are caring for every step of the way. Not letting that individual have a voice in decisions is a tremendous mistake. Many times I have been a total steamroller. It seems I would do anything to roll out a situation and make it smooth. I could have been more flexible. That's one of the bad features of being a strong-headed person! Other parents are perhaps more flexible, but I have seen this frequently with disabled people and their caregivers.

Ron has been through the mill, to use an old expression. He has endured a lot. Another one of my many failures with him is that I concentrated more on Ron's physical condition than on his mental development. I wanted him to be able to face the world better equipped physically. Ron wanted to improve too. He was sixteen and begged me for help to get better. As a result, Ron had a surgical procedure that is not even practiced today in the United States. The operation sounds like something out of a science fiction horror movie. It's called "cryothalamectomy." The procedure involves going into the thalamus, which is located near the top of the brain, with a probe and deadening portions of it by applying extreme cold. The patient is sedated but awake as the electrodes are inserted and the procedure carried out.

Why would anyone have this done? I knew two people who had the operation. One man became a beautiful artist afterwards. The operation didn't improve his speech but it cleared his fine motor skills. I also met a woman who had been helped tremendously. It seemed that by deadening a section of the brain, people with cerebral palsy had a chance to

109

become radically different human beings. I saw this. Ron was aware of it as well.

I researched the operation. I consulted my friend Irene in Baltimore. She wasn't considering this operation for her son. I asked Joe what we should do. He said, "It's your decision."

I wrote to Dr. Phelps, the doctor at the cerebral palsy center in Baltimore where Ron had been treated. Dr. Phelps was against it. He explained that the procedure wasn't proven enough and that the thalamus had too many sections. In a cryothalamectomy the thalamus is semi-eradicated. Certain areas are scarred and the scar tissue becomes inactive. The exact functions of the thalamus are unknown, he emphasized. The information he provided made me question the operation for Ron.

I prayed intensely about it and decided no, we wouldn't do it. When I told Ron my conclusion, I got, "You don't want to help me any more. You don't want me to get better, do you?" He was adamant. We went ahead with the surgery. The operation was done on the left side with him awake during the procedure.

Ron was happy with the results of the first operation which he had in 1961. His speech cleared, and he had far more control over his face so that his presentation was better. Although his walking didn't improve as much as he hoped, he could keep his foot straight, and he stood a lot more erect. His arms didn't improve, but he had less uncontrolled movement on the left side. He could hardly wait for the next operation. Ron felt he'd improve even more after a second operation. The other leg had begun to turn in. He was sure a second operation would correct that. He had to use a brace that tore his skin and wanted to get rid of it. Another factor we constantly had to deal with was the reaction he had to the drugs prescribed for him. They caused everything from sleepiness and stupor to hallucinations and physical effects such as nausea and tremors. Ron had his second surgery about two years later. But this time they put him to sleep completely. He was in a deep coma. Because of that, they couldn't monitor the precise positioning of the needle. I observed the procedure and I was sick about the whole thing. I'll never forget that day. It was so very difficult. His surgery was in the early morning, and he was still unconscious in recovery late that afternoon. I feared he wouldn't come out of the anesthesia at all.

The second surgery was a major disappointment for Ron. He shouldn't have had it. I felt that I had made a big mistake, especially when I saw the results and how it threw things off for him. He suffered from headaches off and on and he became more spastic. In fact, he could never walk decently after the surgery. To him, walking was paramount. The rest wasn't so important.

Things can be really bad, but if you look deep enough you can find some good. At least the first procedure did clear up his facial expressions although his walking went down the tubes. He no longer had any problem with grimaces and drooling. We could understand his speech better. This operation is not done in the United States anymore. In fact, Ron was one of the last patients to have the procedure done with a machine that at the time cost $25,000. We later heard of a woman who had the operation after Ron's. She went into a coma and eventually died.

That day of his second surgery was a gloomy November day in 1963. As I sat waiting for Ron to come out of anesthesia, we heard the tragic news that President John F. Kennedy had been assassinated. It truly was one of the saddest days of our lives.

℘ 19 ℘

Ron's Marriage and Little Ron

R on recuperated from his second cryothalamectomy surgery and adjusted to his new limitations. This was hard, of course, as walking was now more of a challenge for him. He continued taking the bus to school every day. He was much older than the other students because of all the time he missed due to his surgeries and the other difficulties of his condition. But in 1970, at the age of twenty-three, Ron graduated from North High School. He had his graduation picture taken. He looked good in his suit, and we had a party for him. He was ready to begin life as an adult and that meant a job.

Ron started working at MDI (Minnesota Diversified Industries), a company that employs people with disabilities and those who have difficulty working for various reasons. He held a variety of positions related to packaging and mailing. Ron was happy to have a real job and to be earning money. He enjoyed the work but not the low pay.

Ron continued living upstairs at home with us. Mark was going to Lakewood Community College and working at the power company. He bought an old Jeep with those funny plastic windows. In the mornings he'd help Ron climb into it and drive him to his job at MDI. This worked out well. Ron made friends at work. I packed his lunch every-day. He'd either come home by bus or get a ride.

Of course, nothing ever goes smoothly for too long in my life. Something always comes up. I noticed that when Ron was home in the evenings and on weekends he was on the phone a lot. The kids had their own telephone upstairs. I never really asked him about the calls. I figured he was probably chatting with co-workers. I regarded that as a positive development in his life.

One evening Joe and I were at the house of friends for dinner. I always made sure to leave the phone number of where we'd be at home. I got a frantic call from Ron.

"Mom, there's someone from work named Cindy," he began. "Her mother just threw her out of the house. She doesn't have any place to go. She doesn't have any money. Can you and Dad pick her up?"

We didn't know what was going on and, thinking Ron was lend-ing a helping hand to a friend, we drove to Hampden and University Avenues where we picked up Cindy at eleven o'clock at night. She was standing on the street corner with all her worldly goods around her in paper bags—a sad sight. We brought Cindy home and I fixed up a room for her. Ron seemed so relieved and happy to have her at the house. What a caring guy, I thought. And he knows he can count on us.

A few days later we were all talking and trying to figure out what to do. "Cindy," I asked, "why did you mother throw you out? Did you have a fight?"

"Yes, we did."

"A bad one?"

"Yes. She's furious. She doesn't want me to marry Ron and told me not to see him anymore."

Marry Ron? What was going on here? Where had I been? Why didn't I know that my son not only had a girlfriend but was planning to get married?

"What? You want to get married?"

"Yes," they answered.

"We're in love," declared Cindy.

Ron and Cindy in love? That was a shock. Yes, I knew he had been talking on the phone a lot. Obviously it was to just one person—Cindy. And this had been going on for quite a while. They had met at work. They ate lunch together every day. They became close friends, sweethearts. Cindy's mother had gotten wind of the relationship and was beside herself. Cindy was a disadvantaged person who was employed at the MDI workshop as well. She was almost twenty and Ron was now twenty-eight.

Joe sat on the couch with his let's-see-how-you-deal-with-this-one look. Much talk and discussion followed. Neither one of them was capable of any degree of independent living, not physically and certainly not financially. Nor were they capable of a mature approach to their situation.

"What will you do for money?" I asked them.

"I work, Mom. I earn money," Ron answered. He was proud and determined. He wanted a life like anyone else. He was also vulnerable in so many ways.

"But what you both make won't begin to cover the costs of living together," I pointed out.

"We can be on welfare," Cindy said serenely.

It was a very unhappy situation. My daughter Heidi was still at home then. She was a great support during this time.

"What will I do, Heidi? I can't lock them up. They're both of legal age."

"Ron has a right to a life, Mom. Let them get married. Maybe it'll turn out okay and they'll be happy."

"Well, you talk to Cindy about sex, pregnancy, and birth control. Make sure she knows what to do." Heidi even bought Cindy birth control pills.

I contacted a friend who owned a nice large apartment building that was accessible for Ron in Oakdale about three miles from my house.

She helped them make arrangements with the county welfare office. We furnished it for them. At some point, the thought crossed my mind that Cindy was a calculating person who was doing a great job of using Ron for her own purposes.

All my life I've had to make one decision after another—good or bad. This was another one and I felt caught. I asked the good Lord for guidance, but didn't get any.

Our plan was to take Ron and Cindy just over the South Dakota border to be married. Backing out of the driveway in my white Monte Carlo, I had two flat tires. "Ron and Cindy, this is a bad omen," I said. "Are you really sure you want to go through with this?" But they insisted on doing it. They seemed so happy. We had bought Cindy a pretty dress. They had a nice little wedding. Heidi and I were witnesses. We went out for supper and then drove them home.

A few months went by fairly smoothly. Then one night Cindy and Ron both came to the house. They were smiling ecstatically. Before I could offer them anything, they announced that they were having a baby. It was due in the summer. I almost flipped. How would they take care of a baby? As it was, I worried all the time about how they, and especially Ron, were doing. With good reason, I found out.

The baby, Ronald Bruce Junior, arrived August 14, 1977. Ron couldn't get to the hospital for the birth so I drove him the next day. Cindy's mother was there. She wasn't very friendly toward us. Ron was able to see his son at that time. Ronnie Bruce was a cute baby. And my first grandchild. I welcomed him and looked forward to having this wonderful baby as part of the family. However, the reality was that a disabled person was married to an immature person. I saw the relationship unraveling.

Cindy would go out with the baby and not tell Ron where she was going. Sometimes she would leave the baby with other people and tell

115

Ron she had given the baby away. That was mental torture for Ron. Then in midwinter, about six months after the baby was born, I got a late night call from the police.

"Do you have a son named Ron Myers?"

"Yes. What happened?"

"We picked him up on the street without an overcoat on. What should we do with him?"

"Bring him home."

Cindy had locked Ron out of the apartment and wanted nothing more to do with him. Ron stayed with us for a long time. We had to go to court and arrange visitation to see the baby. Then Cindy moved out of town. In order for Ron to see his son, I had to drive to where Cindy was living, pick up Ronnie Bruce and bring him back to our house for the weekend. Ronnie Bruce would say "Truck, truck," and jump in the car for the ride to St. Paul. Cindy picked him up at our house on Sunday nights. Her next move was out of state to where her relatives lived. Again we went to court, but the judge's decision was that she could move wherever she wanted. Her legal expenses were covered by the state, but I had to hire a lawyer to secure Ron's visitation rights.

Ron had a great caseworker who supported him, and she drove him to North Dakota where Cindy was living for a visitation. No one was home. For the next visitation I had to get the sheriff and a court order to bring Ronnie Bruce to my home for a week. Cindy had more children and marriages. A couple of times I sent money and Ronnie Bruce came by bus to visit. He'd stay with us for a few weeks at Ron's place. I hired someone to help out with childcare. But arranging to see him was becoming more and more of a challenge. He was such a sweet, nice child.

When I found out his mother had him on Ritalin, I went to court again. He was extremely agitated in school, and Cindy had a doctor in North Dakota who kept her supplied with pills for him. At court, medical experts gave their opinions disapproving the drug's use for him, but our efforts failed.

On our last visit, when Ronnie Bruce was about eight, we went to a friend's place by the river. It was summer. Together we dug up a little birch tree and planted it in my backyard. Now it's a great big tree. I always have something to remember him by. After that, several years passed before we saw him. When Ronnie Bruce was sixteen, he wanted to come to visit. He was living in North Dakota. His mother had moved back to the Twin Cities, but he stayed on living with his stepfather. Ronnie Bruce was a quiet, withdrawn and very serious young man. Occasionally Ron would hear from his son, but we didn't see him again for twelve years.

The saga of Ron is really something. It takes the cake, as the expression goes. This was one time Joe didn't keep his opinion to himself. "Aileen," he said, "you should have stayed out of this. You shouldn't have let them get married. You just can't say no to Ron. You've never been able to say no to him."

Ouch.

My friend Irene in Virginia whose son has cerebral palsy wasn't much comfort either. "I advised you years ago to have him sterilized," she told me by phone. "If you had taken my advice, you wouldn't be having these problems." She handled things by hiring a prostitute once a month for her son. I just couldn't have had Ron sterilized. I regard fertility as something sacred within a person. To me it would be like an execution. Joe always asked, "Are you sure you're right?" I was sure I was right—and I got all these problems for sticking by my convictions. But I believe in personal freedom, and I couldn't have done it to Ron, disabled or not. He's proud of having a son. Not many disabled people have children of their own.

I also talked this over with my nursing school friend. "What did I do wrong, Julie, and what can I do?" I asked her. She replied, "Just accept it. You can't do it over, you know."

Good advice. One thing I do when I go to bed: I close my eyes, I say my prayers, and all thoughts leave me. I do not dwell on anything. I try not to go back over any of it.

117

ॐ 20 ॐ

Ron Takes on the World

The truth of the matter is that after his break up with Cindy, Ron suffered a severe depression. That was part of the reason I made such an effort to keep in touch with Ronnie Bruce. It was a real heartbreaker for Ron and for all of us.

Fortunately, Ron's life wasn't all doom and gloom. My brother John was living in San Diego. He had married and had a son but had gotten divorced. He invited Ron to fly out to visit. Ron went by himself. But John was late and Ron, traveling as a disabled passenger, was kept at the airport. It was an adventure for him to travel on his own and have to explain his situation to strangers. John finally arrived and picked up Ron who was a little worried but calm. The highlight of the trip for Ron was going to Mexico on the back of John's motorcycle. They went bargain hunting and bar hopping. He assured me they just drank Cokes at the bars.

At least Ron had his job at MDI. Ron was now an inspector. He also moved into a new living facility constructed to accommodate disabled people on the East Side of St. Paul. I bought him a full-sized bed, a dresser and a davenport for his apartment. A homemaker came in for a few hours every morning to help him get dressed and make him breakfast.

118

She also did housework and cooking. He'd wait for Metro Mobility to pick him up and take him to his job.

The workability of this system depended one hundred percent on the people who were assisting Ron. For a time he'd have a responsible person who always showed up, but inevitably things would change and that helpful aide moved or switched jobs. Another aide would sign on— someone with a feeble sense of responsibility who wouldn't arrive on time causing Ron to be late or miss work altogether.

Ron figured he could solve that problem by having a live-in aide. He moved to a place with two bedrooms, one for the aide. The aide he got happened to be a girl who came from an agency. She had a Rottweiler and the dog lived with them. Ron had no control over her or the dog. She let the dog bark. The landlord told Ron he had to manage his aide and her dog or he would be evicted. What a mess. The eviction notice came. He had been there only a few months. I couldn't believe it. He went through so much to find a suitable place and now he was being thrown out through no fault of his own. An eviction would go on his record making it difficult for him to find an apartment in the future.

Fortunately, as a private duty nurse I had taken care of a little boy for two and half years. His father was an attorney who was able to help Ron avoid eviction. "We'll get him a six-month extension and a continuation," the lawyer told me. "But Ron has to fire the aide." Ron did. I figured out that Ron didn't say anything when the aide began causing so much uproar because he was afraid she'd leave, and he would have to start the search for someone all over again.

Getting and holding on to a good aide is worth as much as winning the lottery. In fact, it is a kind of lottery—with about the same chances. One aide said, as he introduced himself, "I'll try working for you, but I'm still looking for another job that pays more. I gotta make my truck payments, ya know." Another person was sent by the agency to work with Ron right off the street with no background check, no training. "I'm just here to see how I like the work," she announced, coolly surveying Ron and his apartment.

119

Then there was the live-in aide named Dawn. She buttered Ron up. He was living over on Rice Street. She'd take him to bars with her. No, she was not trying to improve his social life. I didn't know half of what happened until after the fact. I did tell her to bring Ron over to my house if she wanted time off on weekends. But she'd take him with her to these guys' homes and he'd sleep on the couch while she was with the guy in bed. I also found out Ron was living on beer, pizza, spaghetti and lasagna. That was all she ever gave him. At least he never complained about being bored.

It always griped the daylights out of me that Ron would never say anything. He just absorbed the situation and let it go by. He really fears being left without help. He's become very cautious with his aides. Disabled people become less trusting. They realize that in most instances they can't fight back. It makes them prisoners of a situation. I know that there were times his aides never brought food in or came by to prepare him a meal. He'd have to go to a restaurant if he could get there.

When he lived off Rice Street near downtown St. Paul, this became critical. He had an aide named Jill. She would go off and get drunk and forget to come back. But he wouldn't say a word about her. Don't forget, he was fierce about his independence. One Sunday I went to see him. "Ron, I have some extra food I made," I said. "How about we eat together?"

As we were eating, Jill came in. "What the hell are you doing here?" she demanded. She was weaving drunk.

"You go away till you're sober," I told her walking her to the door. Then she grabbed me and pinned me against the wall. I managed to get free and call 911. The police arrested and booked her, but the agency still wouldn't fire her.

Ron also tried group homes for the disabled. He didn't really like living in them. As he says, they were just buildings, not homes. And he'd see too much of what was going on. Some staff members smoked marijuana, used every drug on the street, and proudly proclaimed the fact that they were only working for money to buy cocaine. I asked Ron if he felt insecure or scared. "I try to deal with it, Mom," he told me, "and just let it go because if I tell anyone or complain, they'll say I'm making it up." A disabled person is at a tremendous disadvantage in such situations.

One time in a group home, his roommate had a seizure and fell out of bed. He got entangled in the bed clothes and was suffocating. Ron pressed the emergency call button but no one responded. Ron set out to get help, pulling himself along the best he could with his walker. He went all over the building looking for someone. He finally found the entire staff in the basement partying. Fortunately his roommate survived, but ever since then Ron has been leery of group homes and prefers to take his chances living on his own. That meant, of course, no shortage of adventures for both of us.

For a while he was living in a rough neighborhood. He liked it because it was accessible to downtown. But there were times I couldn't sleep at night worrying about him. The guys in the neighborhood who knew us called me "Little Mom." I was never bothered when I visited him, but I knew Ron had people smoking marijuana in his apartment. He'd let them come in with drugs. Ron was putting himself in jeopardy all the time. And I'm legally responsible for him. I could have ended up in jail. I finally moved him out. It practically took an act of congress. I got him into an apartment closer to me.

One stormy Saturday night the phone rang about 11:00 P.M. I was already in bed. It was Ron. "Mom, come and get me. I'm over in Minneapolis someplace."

"Is that were Jill takes you when she takes care of that lady?"

"Yes, I'm here. I haven't had anything to eat."

I didn't know the way and I wasn't going to drive to Minneapolis in the middle of the night. "Give me the address, Ron. I'll call a cab to get you and bring you here." That was fifty-two dollars for a cab to pick him up and for the driver to carry him into my house.

Ron likes action. When he's feeling okay, he wants to be where the action is. I understand that. Look at who his mother is! But the reality for a disabled person is tough because it's hard to participate on equal footing, and a disabled person is so much more vulnerable.

Mark had a great idea. He got Ron a police scanner. "Now he'll know what's going on," Mark said. "He can scope out the entire neighborhood."

Ron held his MDI job for about six years. He eventually decided to quit because his assistants were so irregular about coming on time that most days he arrived late or had to miss work altogether. It was too bad. Ron needed to be with others doing something productive. Independence and self-sufficiency then became his goal. He wanted to be on his own and that meant having independent mobility.

"Mom, I think I should get a scooter," Ron told me one day when I was taking him to a doctor's appointment.

"Do you know how much they cost?"

"The one I'd like is about three thousand, but I can get federal funding for a part of that."

Ron had gone on medical assistance at age twenty-one. That paid a large portion of his housing costs, covered his medical needs and paid for his assistants. The amount he received left him with a small food allowance. That was about it. Anything else had to be paid for by his family. That meant me.

When scooters started becoming available for people with disabilities, Ron was immediately interested. Walking had become harder for him and he saw a scooter as giving him the independence he longed for. He could get on and off easily and drive it well. But three thousand dollars for a scooter? This was in the 1980s.

"It's a great idea, Ron, but—" I looked over at him. He had grown a dapper beard that didn't hide the firm set of his jaw. He gazed at me through his large-frame glasses. He had that I-know-you-can-solve-this-Mom expression I knew so well.

"Ron, what am I supposed to do—rob a bank?" I could scrape together only a portion of the money from my savings. But I started my brain going on this and began talking to people. I'm no stranger to raising money. I've joined with other parents of kids with cerebral palsy to raise money for our organization. Finally, the wonderful folks from the Maplewood Veterans of Foreign Wars, Moose Lodge and Lions Club raised almost a thousand dollars to help pay for Ron's scooter. With the scooter, Ron was able to come and go on his own. My next car had to have a lift in the back so I could transport his scooter.

Ron received notice that he was selected for jury duty, so he went to the courthouse. He did this all on his own and got around using his scooter. Ron said he wasn't supposed to discuss the case, but he did tell me about his experience. "I was challenged by the attorney, Mom, but the judge stuck up for me. It's funny, when people look at others, they draw such different conclusions. Just because I don't speak perfectly doesn't mean that I can't think well. We heard the case. Each day we had lunch together across the street. It was a pleasure being on jury duty for that week."

I think Ron was almost sorry when jury duty ended.

As he got into his late thirties and forties, his independence became more and more of a goal for him, especially financial independence. Having and managing money are part of anyone's independence and Ron was no exception. Of course, all this led to some interesting, even dramatic scenarios.

Previously, a personal care attendant or PCA was not required to carry bonding and often had only minimal training. The goal for people on medical assistance is to live as independently as possible and direct their own care with the appropriate assistance of a PCA. That's the ideal. The reality can be quite different.

In 1986 Ron accepted a University of Minnesota student as a live-in attendant who had been approved by the public health nurse and was paid by the state, but no background check was done on him. The attendant set up credit card accounts in Ron's name then used them to pay for his own expenses. He also got Ron to sign blank checks and at other times forged Ron's signature.

I usually oversee Ron's account, but in this case the attendant was pretty crafty. I found out what was going on when I picked up some papers from the bank over at Ron's apartment. "What's happened to your account, Ron? How come you owe all this money to the bank? Who's been helping you with your money?"

"The guy who's my aide," he said and slowly the story came out. "Every time I tried to tell him I thought something was wrong, he'd get mad and I got scared," Ron told me. "I kept thinking he was going to shape up. And I knew that if I lost him that I'd have to deal with the hassle of finding someone else."

It was depressing for him and humiliating to be taken advantage of like that. Such an experience contributes to a feeling of vulnerability and loss of control. Most of us take for granted that we have control over our lives.

We went to court but of course the guy didn't show up. He was a law student and knew what to do. We got a judgment for three thousand dollars against him for forging Ron's name on checks, but he had no assets under his name. We were never able to collect it even though I tried. He must be a smart but crooked lawyer somewhere.

After a law was passed in 1987 by the Minnesota legislature, aides have to be employed by a health care company that meets state standards for bonding, liability insurance and background checks. It still doesn't solve all the problems, but it's a step in the right direction and offers some protection.

I've noticed that several people who have gotten close to Ron seemed to have ulterior motives. He'd lend people money and they'd never pay it back. Case workers and others would talk to him and tell him not to lend the little he has. His response? "Well, if they need it that bad, they can have it."

One of the ongoing puzzles of my life is what exactly Ron understands about money and finances. He either grasps the whole topic way better than I do or he's pretty deficient. Because his schooling was interrupted so frequently by surgeries and other absences due to his disability, I'm sure he missed some important classes in basic math. I don't think he can do numbers or figure out expenses. Add the fact that he's too easily influenced by what he sees on TV and we have the makings of a risky financial situation.

No matter what Ron tries to do, sooner or later it shows up on my radar screen. I may take a while to figure things out, but I generally get to the bottom of it. Another time, I just had this sense that something wasn't adding up. When I got a printout of all his expenses, I thought I would die. Ron had been buying things for himself but a lot of stuff for other people, mainly his aides—nice jewelry, for example. Is he generous, I asked myself, or is he a pushover? Of course, it was all done with credit cards. He had been paying off a small amount each month but he owed over six thousand dollars—and this was twenty years ago. He could never pay that off with his medical assistance allowance. I had no way of knowing how much his aides were involved in these purchases either.

I went to see Stan, my friend Julie's husband, the attorney.

"What should I do? I don't have the money to pay off his debts."

"It looks like declaring bankruptcy is your only option," he said.

"How am I going to pay for that?"

"You can do it on your own. Get the forms, fill them out and file them at the courthouse. If you have any questions, call me."

"Good Lord, do I really deserve this?" I asked him. "I have other kids at home. I'm working and managing a house, and on top of everything I have to go downtown to the courthouse to fill out all the paperwork for bankruptcy court?"

"If anyone can do it, you can," Stan reassured me.

The day of the hearing, Ron and I arrived at court. As we were waiting our turn, Ron said, "Look, Mom, the other people have real attorneys with briefcases, not their moms carrying folders stuffed with papers."

"You're lucky to have me. Be glad I didn't bring a grocery bag with all your credit card receipts. We just need to get this done. Don't forget, you dragged me into this."

125

Fortunately, the judge sized up the situation and allowed him to declare bankruptcy.

I asked Ron, "Why do you charge things when you know you don't have the money to pay for them?"

"Well, I figure some day I'll have the money," he said. "Besides, everybody else does it."

For some reason the stock market has always fascinated Ron. I don't understand how someone without any money could be so drawn to it. At some point he decided he was going to invest in stocks. He found a broker at Schwab who has a son with cerebral palsy and they became friends. So he calls his contact for advice and to discuss things. Ron won't tell anyone his stockbroker's name. I think Ron's dream was to get rich in the stock market or something. He'd buy and sell, but even with the small fees at Schwab, Ron never made much money. That's good because with medical assistance, he has a three thousand dollar limit. But I think knowing that he has a few stocks here and there helps him feel equal to others.

Our cerebral palsy group had gatherings where our kids and other disabled people can get together. At one time there were a lot of events and we'd take Ron but pretty much against his will. He really didn't want to participate. Joe would say to Ron, "Make your mother happy and just go." But he wasn't interested in being with other disabled people. He always appeared quite uncomfortable in these groups. It seems that psychologically he wants to erase that portion of his life. Or perhaps it has more to do with the fact that he appreciates people with experience in the world who talk to him like a regular person. He wants relations with people like the relationship he has with his stockbroker friend at Schwab.

I wonder, if Ron hadn't had cerebral palsy would he have been a stockbroker?

Aileen and her mother, Nettie Haugen Ekstrom.   Aileen with her father, John William Ekstrom

Aileen Helen Ekstrom at age two.

Aileen (middle with braids), her sister Edna Karin and cousin Florence.

Aileen with her horse on the family farm in Towner, North Dakota.

Aileen's graduation from high school, 1931.

Aileen and Nightingale, the horse she rode while living in Seattle.

Graduation portrait, St. Luke's School of Nursing, 1935.

Aileen serving as a member of the Minnesota National Guard.

Portrait of Aileen in her twenties.

Aileen and her first husband Everett "Bud" Myers.

Ron, his grandmother and Aileen's blue Crosley.

Ron in Towner, North Dakota.

Ron and his grandmother.

Aileen and Ron.

Aileen worked as an industrial nurse at 3M in the 1950s.

Ron in grade school portrait.

Birthday party for Ron.

Aileen and Joe.

Aileen Fritsch.

Ron with his first scooter partly funded by the Maplewood
Veterans of Foreign Wars, Moose Lodge and Lions Club.

Ron rescued the family dog, Kat, and
reported a fire at the house by crawling
to a neighbor's.

Aileen and her family: Greg and Heidi Rastetter, Ron, Mark, Aileen and Joe with Kat.

The scene at Skydive Twin Cities after Aileen's jump. On the scooter is her son Ron. Right, Kerry McCauley, co-owner of Skydive Twin Cities. Far right is Mark Fritsch, Aileen's other son.

Aileen, her skydiving partner Kerry McCauley, and all of Aileen's family who came for the jump and her birthday celebration.

๑ 21 ๖

On the Road with Aileen

Given my love of adventure and travel, I jumped at any chance to get away whenever I could. This trait also showed up in my brother John, younger than me by nine years. He was a real vagabond. At age sixteen he left home with a buddy of his. He spent time in Nevada and worked setting dynamite in mines. But no matter where he was, he always phoned my mom every Sunday night. Never missed. After he married, he lived in San Diego where I visited him several times.

Once, when the kids were young, Joe's aunt came from North Dakota to visit. I took off to see John. I went with him on the back of his chopper all down the coast of Baja California. That was a great time. I never told Joe about the motorbike trip, though!

I did, however, come back with a Mexican-style glass lampshade. I had it all padded and wrapped up to carry on board with me, but the airline agent stopped me and said it had to be checked as luggage.

"Why?" I asked. "People bring other things on board."

"You can only carry on things you wear, like hats and coats."

So I went back to my brother and he helped me unwrap the lampshade. I put it on my head and walked past the agent onto the airplane.

"Isn't this stylish?" I said to the stewardess as I settled in my seat. Then I gave her a few dollars and asked if she could put it someplace safe for me.

When we arrived back in Minnesota, I put it on my head again and strolled off the plane. My kids thought I was nuts.

In 1972 Joe and I took our first trip to Europe together. We flew into Zurich. We had a wonderful visit. He showed me all the places in Switzerland where he grew up and we met members of his family. My hair is originally brown and still is, but when I went to the West Coast to work years ago, I started dying my hair blond—blondes have more fun, right?—and decided that was me. The only time I regretted that decision was on our return to the U.S. We were waiting to board the plane in the Zurich airport when suddenly I was pulled out of the line and marched off into a back room. There I was strip searched and grilled about my activities—what had I done on the trip, what was I bringing back, who had I seen. They were not one bit friendly to me. They went through all my clothes. Finally they said I could get dressed and leave. It turns out I fit the profile of a known drug carrier perfectly. I asked to see a picture of the woman. They showed it to me. We looked exactly alike, same build and same blond hair.

Joe didn't know what had happened to me. The plane was held for forty-five minutes. Everyone booed at me when I got on the plane. Why do all these weird things happen to me!

My friend Dorothy and I went on a cruise through the Gulf of Mexico to Colombia. We had the option of staying overnight at a charming resort on the beach. For some reason, though, we decided to remain on the cruise ship. Our stateroom faced the port and we noticed small motor boats scooting back and forth from the shore to a ship beyond the three-mile limit. Later that night the army came in and raided the resort looking for drugs, but they didn't find anything because the resort owners had been tipped off.

Every summer we'd take a two-week vacation to a resort along the White Fish Lake chain in northern Minnesota. But when Mark graduated from high school in 1975, we went on a trip with the entire family that was the highlight of all our trips. We rented a Winnebago. I had saved and saved for this. Besides paying the rental, I had to give them my life savings, it seemed, as a deposit. We took our dog with us even though we had to pay duty on her when we went to Canada.

The night before we left was Mark's graduation party. I took every bit of food from his party and packed it in the Winnebago's huge refrigerator—ham, turkey, potato salad—I gathered up everything. I shook out the tablecloth to leave the crumbs for the birds and we took off in the morning. We didn't have to buy any food for a long time.

Our first stop was Mount Rushmore in the Black Hills of South Dakota. Ron and Mark went up in a helicopter to view the sculptures of the presidents. Ron thought the helicopter ride was "kind of scary," though Mark liked it.

We never drove at night. At about four or five o'clock, we usually pulled into a KOA Campgrounds of America, otherwise we wouldn't get a space. The KOA had shower stalls that we had to put money in to use. I'd go with Heidi, and Joe would go with the boys. Some camps even had swimming pools.

The dog would sit up all night in the driver's seat in the Winnebago. If there were any problems or if anyone walked too close to the Winnebago, she'd beep the horn to alert us. She'd be so tired out from guarding us that she'd sleep all day. Her name was "Kat Ballou" from the 1965 Western featuring Lee Marvin and Jane Fonda. The dog's name invariably caused confusion at the vet's.

It was a really nice, roomy Winnebago with two swing hammocks that Mark and Heidi used. Ron slept on the davenport and there was a double bed in back. We didn't have to worry about where Kat slept because she was on duty in the driver's seat all night. I'd see the dog up there, her head moving, following the activity outside the camper.

We went through Yellowstone up into Canada to Banff and Lake Louise. It was gorgeous country. Just beautiful. Then we crossed to the West Coast where I had relatives in Seattle—my cousins from my early nursing days. We drove down to California and did the whole Fisherman's Wharf thing in San Francisco. The kids were fascinated. Back then Ron could walk holding on to someone, so we walked everywhere. We also went to the San Francisco Zoo. Joe's birthday was June 22nd. We celebrated with a birthday cake that had those candles that you can't blow out. We had a lot of fun with that.

We camped for a day in Big Sur. That was quite an experience. We shared the camp with long-haired hippies dressed in colorful clothes and wearing handmade pendants. They came by to say hi, offer us food and check us out. It was the kids' first introduction to a different culture. They had seen hippies and counterculture types in Minnesota, but nothing like this large group of young people sitting around the campfire and listening to music. They danced and sang until late into the night, then just slept out in the open on blankets. We had taken a pup tent along, so when the kids said they wanted to sleep outside like the others, I said fine. But they had to pitch the tent close to the Winnebago. "We'll know when you move," I told them, "because we have invisible strings on you."

Joe asked me, "Why in the world did we come here?"

"I thought it would be an experience for them."

"It certainly is an experience."

The kids eventually decided to come inside. I guess they must have had enough of the culture.

Actually, my plan had been to stop at a regular campground that we knew of through the American Automobile Association, but we arrived too late and couldn't get in, so we ended up at a free recreational area that was completely taken over by hippies. Joe called them "yippies." The experience appealed to me. I've never been a cautious person.

We went on to San Diego where my brother lived. After spending two days at his place, we drove into Mexico. John came with us but he rode his chopper and gave the kids rides. They loved that.

Everyone, including me, seemed to forget about my birthday on June 27th so I claimed to be a year younger. But Joe wanted to surprise me by arriving in Las Vegas to celebrate. Joe and Mark drove over 100 MPH to get us there while the rest of us slept. We parked in one of the huge Stardust Casino lots. Everybody else went to the casino while I got ready to go to a show later that evening with Joe. Suddenly Heidi burst in the door out of breath. "Mom, the guard at the casino wouldn't let me go in with the others. He said I was too young and made me leave," she said. "I couldn't find the Winnebago. All these strange people were out there and someone was following me." I was furious that Joe hadn't brought her back. To this day, Heidi refuses to go to Las Vegas.

On our way back home we visited Pike's Peak and Denver. We did the drive home pretty fast. Joe was tired. He, Mark, and I had to get back to work. And I was running out of Winnebago-kitchen cooking ideas.

All in all we traveled over 1,700 miles and were gone about six weeks. When I had told Julie my plans, she said I'd lost my mind completely. But looking back, I never doubted this would be a great experience for us.

Once on a trip to the East coast with Joe, he took me to the neighborhood where he had lived in New Jersey. I had never been there before, but as we passed one particular house, I had a very strange feeling. "Joe," I said, "I've been in this house before. I know what the house is like inside. It has a big window that overlooks the backyard. Let's see if anyone is home." Joe looked at me with his what-is-she-up-to-now expression, but before he could say anything, I rang the doorbell. The owners of the house were home. I explained that we were visiting Joe's old neighborhood. We started chatting and they invited us inside—into a sitting room in back with a picture window. They had owned the house for thirty years. I didn't say anything more about my strong déjà vu feeling. Joe was a little spooked.

One summer afternoon I was at home not doing too much. I was sixty-five at the time. Mark came by on his motorcycle.

"Hi, Mom. I just stopped in to say good-bye," he said. He was on his way to New York to see his half-brother Paul. "My friend who was going with me can't make it." I know Mark hadn't planned on taking me, but he said, "I've got room on my bike and an extra helmet. Want to come? We can split the gas."

It took me all of two seconds to decide to go. "Let me throw together my things." I gathered my knitting, a good book, my makeup, some clothes, a warm jacket, cash, and a foam pad. "Ready," I said. We stashed my stuff, I settled onto the foam pad, put my arms around Mark's waist, and we took off. Mark made fun of the foam pad. He thought it looked funny.

He wanted to get there in two days, so we traveled pretty hard. Our first stop was in Indiana after 650 miles straight. I heard good music coming out of a bar across from our motel. "Mark," I announced, "I'm going dancing." Mark could barely walk. He went to bed. The next day Mark asked me for a piece of the foam I was sitting on. He said "If it kept you in good enough shape to dance all night after 650 miles of traveling, then I sure could use it."

To pass the time as we rode along, I'd pull out my book or get in some knitting.

As we neared New York, we saw a motorcycle gang stopped under a bridge in front of us. They were smoking and doing drugs. We were on a less-traveled road and had to pass right through the gang and their motorcycles. Mark figured they would jump us. We had to stop. I got off the back of the bike, took off my helmet, pulled out a cigarette and walked over to them. "Got a light?" I asked.

"Huh? Oh, sure. Sure, lady."

Soon I was chatting with these tough-looking, leather-clad guys lounging on their big bikes. They waved to us as we went on our way. I don't think Mark's heart stopped thudding until we got to the next county.

We ran into some heavy rain on the way. I noticed a car following us almost protectively. We pulled into a rest stop and I went to the ladies' room. In came a woman. "We were so worried about you kids in the storm," she said. She nearly fainted when I took off my helmet. I told her I was traveling with my son. She and her husband were much younger.

In Rockefeller Center, I regaled folks with stories of our adventures. We visited all our relatives in New York. I think they still haven't gotten over what Mark and I did.

၈ 22 ရ

Syria

One of my all-time great trips was to Syria in 1984. That was an especially rich trip and a continual history lesson. It came about because of Marge and Larry Chambers, longtime friends from Towner, North Dakota, who had gone to Syria on a two-year United Nations project. When they came to St. Paul to visit their daughter Debbie, I invited them all over for dinner. The entire evening they talked about Syria. I was totally fascinated. In September they would be back in Syria for their last year, and they asked me if I'd like to visit them along with their daughter Debbie. I was delighted. I sensed it would be a memorable experience.

Just making plans for our trip that evening gave me a wonderful feeling. I knew Deb would be a good traveling companion. How lucky can you be! I hurried to get my visa, which took a while because the Syrian embassy checked all previous travel, and if you had gone to the Holy Land, they would not issue you a visa. I knew it would be hot most of the time so no heavy clothes. Of course I packed my trusty hot water bottle that I always travel with because inevitably there are cold nights. I believe in creature comforts. That's first on my list.

We flew to Frankfurt where we stayed overnight. Next morning we took a flight to Syria with Lufthansa Airlines. However, on the way to Syria, the plane ran short of fuel and had to stop in Cypress. Not a comfortable stop. During the hour-long refueling, the air conditioning was turned off. Cypress was hot and it was stifling in the plane. We had to stay on board while soldiers marched around the plane shooting their guns in the air. However, the German stewards kept filling everyone's glasses with whiskey. Needless to say, by the time we arrived in Damascus, Syria, I was quite happy and oblivious to discomfort

I noticed that the women who had come aboard in Frankfurt were beautiful and very elegantly dressed. They went to the restrooms and when they came out, they were wearing long black jilaabah or cloaks with veils that covered their faces. Only their gorgeous shoes were visible. I love shoes so I caught that!

I spoke to the women who told me they had been on holiday in Paris with their husbands. I'm not nosy, just inquisitive. I told them who I was and what I did and they told me about themselves. It was so interesting to meet them.

When we walked off the plane in Damascus, soldiers were lined up on either side of us with guns drawn. We had to walk between them to get into the airport. Maybe it was a good thing I had consumed all that whiskey because walking by the soldiers didn't bother me too much. I could have faced wild tigers without a problem. Finally we showed our credentials and there, on the other side of the iron fence, were Marge and Larry waiting for us. They took us by car to the hotel where Debbie and I slept really well.

Syria was full of sights and sounds that were strange to me. The open windows don't have screens on them. But there were no flying bugs either. Our hotel was a French hotel—the Meriden. From our hotel window we could see a military complex. Soldiers were all over. Despite that, we relaxed by the pool and in the courtyard.

144

We visited the impressive Omayyad Mosque where we had to remove our shoes and put on a black cloak. The floor was far from sanitary as it was covered with pigeon droppings. But I did all this for a sight I'd never see again. I truly felt transported to an entirely different world. We heard the Muslim call to prayer from the top of the mosque five times a day. I was told it was played by tape recorder.

All the streets led to a round-about. In this circle there were scaffolds where prisoners convicted of rape and murder were hung until their bodies disintegrated. A body had just been taken down so we didn't see one. For lesser crimes, fingers and toes were cut off. Punishment was swift and brutal. But there were no locks on any of the doors or windows. Quite different from the U.S. Actually, they had few prisoners and very little crime. I can see why. It was a very safe place. People openly wore gold jewelry.

Every building had a door-sized portrait of the president, Hafez al-Assad, hanging on it. Impossible to forget who is in charge! In Damascus there was only one government-owned radio and TV station. American shows dubbed in Arabic were broadcast at one o'clock every afternoon.

I felt I could have spent days in Damascus and never run out of things to see. They had such beautiful art. We visited the souk—the commercial quarters or shop. In this case it was three doors down a narrow street and seemed carved out of rock. Although the shop seemed very primitive, workmen were creating beautiful inlaid mosaics on tables. I watched two men with slender metal tweezers assemble an intricate mosaic. They used goat glue! I picked out a table to bring back with me. I knew I would treasure it at home. I bought it early on while I still had some money.

Speaking of money, I didn't exchange my dollars at the official rate because I knew I'd lose. But I needed cash so one night Larry and I drove down a dark alley. "There will be a guy riding a bike," Larry told me. "He'll go past my car two times. If I beep the horn, he will wait for me." I understood that just fine. A little shady, but I needed the money.

145

I had my U.S. dollars pinned to my bra with a big safety pin right through the bills. I carried the same amount on both sides. But I couldn't open the pin. So there we were in the car in this dark alley with Larry trying to open the safety pin on my bra.

I had a very unexpected and powerful experience when we went to the house said to be where the Apostle Paul stayed after his conversion on the road to Damascus. That appears in chapter nine of the Acts of the Apostles. Paul intended to arrest the followers of the Way, as the early disciples of Jesus were called, and bring them back to Jerusalem in chains. He saw a bright light and heard the voice of Jesus asking him why he was persecuting him. When Paul picked himself up off the ground, he was blind. The men in his entourage had to take him by the hand and guide him into the city. Somehow he found himself at the house of a believer and there, three days later, he was cured of his blindness by Ananias.

It's a simple house with thick walls. When I stepped inside, I was overwhelmed by a sensation so strong that I felt totally unreal. I wasn't myself. It seemed I was witnessing a group of soldiers coming to the door with Paul. I have no idea what this was. Being an old-fashioned Lutheran from North Dakota, I could hardly believe it. I had never felt anything like this before. I thought I was on another planet. I really and truly did. The feeling left me only when I went outside and had a cigarette.

I asked Larry and Marge about it. They said they didn't feel anything but noticed that I was very pale. Something happened. I've always felt I've lived before, but I'm not sure if that was it or just the power of the place. I don't know, but I guess it takes some dumb North Dakota farm girl to feel it.

From Damascus we drove to Aleppo. The roads were very well kept but not heavily traveled. On the road to Aleppo we passed the town of Hama. It had been the center of the fundamentalist Sunni Muslim

146

Brotherhood. This group carried out actions against the government of Hafez al-Assad. The government's response was to shell the city in February of 1982. The assault went on for three weeks, killing tens of thousands and wiping out most of the town. As we passed by it, a little more than two years after the attack, we saw that it was totally leveled. Many who lived there—men, women, children, and animals—were wiped out and the area was paved over with concrete.

The UN project was based near Aleppo. Larry had gotten into this project in Syria because, besides working for the *Mouse River Journal*, Towner's newspaper (that local paper is still being published, by the way), Larry was also an agronomist. In Syria they worked with the Food and Agriculture Organization of the United Nations Development Program project called ICARDA—International Center for Agricultural Research in Dry Areas. The focus of the project was on slowing desert erosion through propagating and planting trees and crops that would keep the land from eroding. During the previous year, the Chambers worked with the Syrians to plant a bean similar to the chick pea that grows easily in arid conditions. The trees they planted were a type of evergreen with long, spreading roots that anchor the soil and provide shade. They were planted in the provinces and people were trained to care for the trees. Everywhere I went, I saw people carrying goatskin bags to water the trees. All this was done under an agreement with the government of Hafez al-Assad. These dry and arid regions in Syria have severe windstorms, so the work of Larry and others at the international research center was very important.

The group working at the center was made up of couples from many different countries. Debbie, who was twenty-six, and I were the oddballs. The conversations at the gatherings revolved around their work and other international experiences. It was exciting to meet these people.

The Chambers and others of the group lived in Shamba, a lovely area with many large trees and paved walkways. The street lights lit up the night like daytime and gave it a fairyland feeling. Every three days someone came to drain and refill the pool. There was no filtration system for the pool. A wrought iron white fence encircled it and the court-yard. From there I could watch the workmen across the way using chis-els and old-world tools to create a beautiful building out of rock.

The toilets were like bidets that gave you a wash when you finished. The only problem was that the force of the water was so strong, it almost knocked me off the pot. I got soaking wet until I learned how to man-age it. The water was always cold.

From Aleppo we went on trips out into the heart of the desert. We vis-ited the city of Palmyra, built around springs. Located on a caravan route, it supported many stable settlements over the centuries. Long ago people lived there in caves. Excavations in 1955 showed that an ancient hunting community had lived at the oasis fifty thousand years ago. It's said that King Solomon reigned over the region. The beautiful architec-ture is attributed to the long occupation by the Roman army. Palmyra is also known for its monumental funerary carvings. Structures are still intact due to the low humidity in the desert. In other areas, the shifting sands have buried entire cities. However, Greek archeologists were mak-ing discoveries. We watched them as they worked meticulously brushing off the sand. It's tedious work, but how fascinating! I could have stayed in Syria for years.

The people, without exception, were friendly. They were happy to see Americans back then. The Bedouins, desert people, are smart—they pitched their goatskin tents around an electric pole and tapped into the electricity.

Huge groves of olive trees surround the bodies of water at the oases. The sky was clear during my entire stay and at night in the desert the stars were so bright, it was almost like daytime.

We traveled in a car with the United Nations ICARDA symbol on it and international license plates. One time we were waved over at an inspection point. Larry was alarmed. But all they wanted was a cigarette lighter. I had several extra so I gave them two and made the soldiers happy. I never had my hands kissed so many times in my life. I told Larry that my cigarettes were a bond between nations. Larry said he figured they must have smelled my cigarette smoke from far off.

It was the custom for the international families working at the Center to take turns hosting dinner parties that featured their traditional food. The host family also wore their national dress. Although I didn't quite like some of the foods, it was always an enjoyable occasion. Everyone was friendly and extremely articulate.

Soon it was the Chambers' turn to host a dinner party. All their food had to be imported from Denmark. We planned a menu of typical U.S. foods. For dessert we were going to make a large frosted cake, so we needed two packages of yellow cake mix. When we emptied them into the mixing bowl, we found little black bugs in both boxes. Those two cake mixes were all we had. "Oh my," exclaimed Marge, "I don't have any dessert. You can't just run out to the grocery store here. And the guests are coming in a few hours."

I stirred the yellow cake mix with the poppy seed-sized bugs in it.

"What are you thinking, Aileen?"

"The truth? Those bugs are all dead and if they aren't, they'll be dead after being baked in the oven. Add the other ingredients, stir it up, and let's bake the cake."

"Well, you're a nurse. You should know."

"Don't worry, Marge. No one will be harmed. Just don't eat any cake."

We put a real thick frosting on it. The cake was lovely and the guests at the dinner party enjoyed it. Now, whenever I see yellow cake, I think about that dinner party.

Even my inlaid mosaic table had a travel adventure. I brought it back with me in my leather suitcase. The legs unscrewed from the top so I packed it securely with all my extra clothes and the print linen wrap-around skirts I had bought, and then I checked my bag. When we left Damascus, we flew to Frankfurt and stayed overnight. But our plane went to Boston the next morning instead of New York where our suitcases had gone. When we got back to Minnesota, no one was in the airport and the carousels were closed. Finally we spotted our suitcases sitting off by themselves, undisturbed. I had wrapped dental floss around the locks so I knew it hadn't been opened. My table arrived in perfect condition. When I got it home, I had a glass top made to protect the delicate mosaic from moisture. I enjoyed it and my memories of Syria so much over the years.

ॐ 23 ॐ

China

All my life I've been drawn to places that piqued my curiosity and fed my love of adventure. Sometimes it seems that curiosity and adventure are the main forces in my life! I was a member of League of Women Voters of St. Paul for many years as part of my quest for answers in the world of politics. I wanted to understand the whys and wherefores of what was going on around us, where we were heading and how national and international events affected us. So when I heard about a three-week trip to China offered through the Minneapolis League of Women Voters, I applied.

I was really excited to get the information packet about the trip. Even the pre-departure meetings with my tour companions were an adventure. It was an interesting group of women who were engaged in many different activities and pursuits. I was the only traveler from St. Paul. It was a remarkable trip because it was arranged by the All-China Women's Federation, the first organization of women acknowledged by the Chinese government. We were one of the few groups from the United States to be invited by them. This was before travel to China was as common as it is now and before the Chinese tourist industry began accommodating Western tourists.

After assembling in San Francisco, we left on a Japan Airlines flight to Tokyo April 15 of 1987. I was pleasantly surprised by the care and attention we received on our Japanese flights. The flight attendants babied us. We had our choice of all shapes and sizes of pillows. We had comfy foot rests, endless hot towels, and back massages. Meals were offered with such grace. We felt very special. I had never experienced this level of care on other international flights.

Our overnight stay in Tokyo included an earthquake. My roommate Dorothy and I were on the twelfth floor and nearly fell out of our beds! We decided this was a sure sign our trip was going to be interesting.

The next morning as we were settling into the bus that would take us to the airport for the flight to Beijing, I realized I had left my well-traveled, trusty hot water bottle in my hotel room. Everyone had to wait while I went back to retrieve it. Because the elevators were so slow, I ran up to the room—all twelve flights. To give my hot water bottle some status in the eyes of my traveling companions, I decided to name it Andy. From then on, they'd check with me on Andy's whereabouts.

Representatives from the Women's Federation welcomed us upon our arrival in Beijing. They planned our trip to include educational stops at orphanages, daycare centers, senior housing, schools, hospitals, factories, and the like. Wherever we went, we were greeted and treated. Our backpacks, provided by the Federation, proclaimed that we were their guests. It was an honor for the Minneapolis League of Women Voters. They also planned sightseeing and cultural activities for us. We had a delightful interpreter and tour guide, Mr. Wu. He spoke excellent English and enriched our tour with his knowledge and insights. Mr. Wu had been a college professor, but due to political changes he was working as a tour guide.

Beijing's phenomenal sights often gave me visions of the country's vast history. Seeing buildings that hadn't changed since the time of the emperors carried me back in history and swept away my sense of the modern present. My son Mark had given me a nice German camera and I busied myself with it. It kept me focused!

One of our stops was Tiananmen Square. Little did we know that two years later it would be the site of the revolt that changed China's political direction. Principally students and educated people were involved in the bloody uprising. Who can forget the scenes of army tanks running over protestors? We visited the university and met many professors and students who would later participate in the uprising. Time would prove that their courage and sacrifices made for change in China.

While in Beijing we saw part of the Great Wall, the fortification around the city. We would see more of the wall as we traveled north. Our two days in Beijing were spent in constant sightseeing. It was great having Mr. Wu as our guide to explain it all. His love and respect for his homeland were evident, and his education and experience in Europe enriched what he told us.

Next we flew to Xi'an for two nights where we stayed in an area rich in history and architecture. The highlight there proved to be the terracotta warriors who faithfully stood guard for two thousand years. It was a sight I will never forget. Even now they are vivid to me. It's amazing how they have lasted so long. I touched one—it felt like steel. We stayed there for another full day to marvel at this area where time seemed to stand still. I noticed that even though we all had watches, no one paid attention to time. It was an odd feeling—as if the world had stopped.

We ate in typical Chinese restaurants that served only one type of food in small amounts on each plate. No overeating was possible. I really enjoyed the tea at each meal and the rice with hot broth over it. I had packed a lot of dried fruit and nuts so I could munch on those. Not many fruits were available. I never noticed any orchards where we traveled. One evening we were served what looked like cooked baby onions and even seemed to smell like onions. I asked Mr. Wu, our faithful guide, what it was. "This is a great Chinese delicacy," he said. "Baby snake eggs." Needless to say, I didn't eat them. I was no longer hungry. Each morning we had what Mr. Wu said was an American breakfast with scrambled eggs and toast with spiced honey and tea. My husband had given me a bottle of Crown Royal brandy and a nip of that really finished off the day for Dorothy and me. I tried to drink Chinese wine but it was too bitter for me. After a busy day of constant moving about, I'd slip into bed with Andy, my faithful hot water bottle, and sleep like a baby. Accommodations, while not luxurious, were always clean and comfortable.

All the while I was busy taking pictures. Even now I enjoy them. China seemed so peaceful then. There was little hint of all the tragic things that would happen or the frenzy of development that would overtake so much of the country. The people were delightful. Many spoke English so we chatted often. We were asked lots of questions, especially by the young. I heard an underlying discontent bothering the young people, especially in urban areas. They couldn't see any progress. As we traveled north into the countryside, we noted that there was less discontent. People seemed adapted to the old system with a certain degree of comfort.

It would be interesting to see how people's demeanor has changed now. I noticed then that people seemed so stoic, as if they were afraid to show emotion. We were treated very well on our trip and had a great deal of freedom. Someone from the Women's Federation checked in with us from time to time to see how things were going. Every place we went they had been there ahead of us to tell them we were coming.

Dorothy and I found it easy to talk to people and had lots of opportunities because we'd stop to smoke. We made all kinds of friends. Groups would form around us. "Take me to America," they'd say. We had a lot of fun with them. They probably hadn't seen many American women standing on a street corner smoking.

"You are American," they'd say to me.

"No, I'm Scandinavian." They had never heard of Scandinavians. "Who are they?"

"They eat fish and have blond hair."

People liked my blond hair. "Why do you have blond hair?"

"From eating fish," I'd tell them.

Next was Nanjing in the foothills of the Purple and Gold Mountains, known for its greenery, broad boulevards and many parks with numerous waterfalls. We visited the Sun Yat-sen Mausoleum, the Taiping Kingdom History Museum which houses artifacts of the Taiping Rebellion, and viewed the Yangtze River from the bridge. The exteriors of these buildings were extremely ornate. I felt I could have spent hours just studying the facades. Then there were centuries-old paintings, sculptures, vases and incredible artwork. The famous jade burial suit was on display at the Jiangsu Provincial Museum. I can't imagine how many years it took to put it together. Mr. Wu gave a detailed description of how intricate the work was. Jade requires very skilled workers. We watched them carve deftly using sharp drills. At the museum shop I bought a small jade bird with a crown of feathers carved from a solid piece of jade.

Wuxi is a popular resort city with landscapes, pavilions, fountains and gardens including the Li Garden on Lake Tai. We went by train and found ourselves in a magical place lit with lanterns at night. We saw a boat made of ivory that an empress had commissioned for herself. What a different life!

We went to a mulberry farm where we met the silk worm mothers. These women live right there all the time and nurture the caterpillars that live and feast on the mulberry trees. When the cocoons are finished, the women pick them and put them into hot water to kill the larvae. The silk is then carefully rolled off and put on large spools. I bought some beauti-

155

ful silk material at the government store. They were very happy to accept my credit card. For other things purchased in the markets, we had to pay with cash. I bought pink silk fabric for the dress I was planning to have made for Mark's wedding. A very clever neighbor of mine sewed it for me. I also bought novel Chinese toys for the children in my family.

We then traveled to Suzhou by boat—a very elaborate boat with couches sporting handmade crochet coverings for the seats and backs. The trip along the river was calm and beautiful. I noticed especially the bamboo growing right along the river's edge.

Next we traveled by train to Shanghai where supposedly fashion styles are set. What's made there is considered the best. It was spectacular. People's Park was immaculate. Mornings in the park we saw old men carrying wooden cages with songbirds inside. They waved the cages to exercise the birds. They claimed this stimulated the birds' singing ability. I was reminded of my grandmother and her songbirds. Apparently the personal touch is essential all over the world.

We stayed overnight in a modern hotel with great accommodations. The old town was in sharp contrast to the very modern new city. Even the people seemed different. Many wore western garb. It was rare to see the Chinese clothing customarily worn then. Bikes were everywhere and wherever there was an open space, someone was doing Tai Chi. There was so much to see at the Shanghai Museum of Art and History. The Jade Buddha Temple of carvings was indescribably beautiful.

We then flew to Guilin and stayed two nights in this enticing place and we cruised down the Li River taking in its inspiring beauty.

Another flight took us to Guangzhou, the main industrial and foreign trade center in south China. What a rude awakening. The city lacked the beauty of the other cities we had seen and it was very westernized—a real contrast to the natural beauty we had come to expect. We visited a factory that produced cloisonné. It's beautiful but, oh, the fumes. The entire city was thick with pollution. Horrible chemicals pollute the water. I don't see how people can live there. My eyes were red and burning from the fumes. It's a good thing I had eye drops along. I used them all of the time. Pictures of Beijing today are what Guangzhou was like twenty years ago. It's a disaster for the people and the environment.

Wherever we went we were treated to cultural events held in extraordinarily beautiful buildings. We saw Madam Butterfly at the Chinese Opera. At a theatre in Red Square we had front row seats. Love of culture is taught early. At the schools we visited, little children played violins almost as big as they were.

We went by train to Hong Kong. The picturesque scenery helped erase the grimness of industrialized Guangzhou. We were told Hong Kong was a shopper's paradise, especially at night. This must be where the phrase "Shop 'til you drop" was coined. We took time to see the island and houseboats of two and three levels.

For our last night we went to Victoria Park to watch the sunset and have dinner. We took a tram that seemed to go straight up. The restaurant rotated slowly while we absorbed the magnificent views. At that dinner we toasted the memory of our China trip. The next day we retraced our route to San Francisco and home to Minnesota. I relived my trip with my photos and unpacking and finding places for my beautiful purchases!

I was saddened by the terrible earthquake which hit the Sichuan province of southwest China. I'm sure they felt it in Xi'an where we had visited. I also watched the 2008 Olympic Games in China with great interest. Having been to China, I feel I have a better understanding of the country and the news from there which I follow with great interest.

↗ 24 ↖

A Dog Named Kat and Other Family Stories

As I've said, my family did a good job of keeping me busy. They were also good at supplying plenty of action and adventure on their own.

One night while I was working a private duty job, Ron had a chance to prove himself. Joe and Ron were home alone. Usually Ron went to bed by eight, but because he had the next day off from work, he was up that evening. Joe began heating something on the stove, then went to the basement. A fire started. Ron smelled the smoke and called out to Joe, but Joe didn't hear him. Because Ron couldn't use a dial phone, he had to go to the neighbor's house across the driveway. Ron managed to get himself and the family dog outside. Then he crawled to Tina's house, banged on the door and had her call the fire department. He was featured in the local paper and got a lot of attention. Ron, however, just said, "My mom taught me to be calm and cool and to think about what I have to do. So that's what I did and I made it to the neighbor's."

Mark liked to go caving. Early one season when it was still cold, he went into a horseshoe cave during a Boy Scout camping trip and got stuck. The parka he was wearing wouldn't let him move forward or go back. He told me he was pretty nervous as he tried to wriggle free. He finally slipped out of his jacket and crawled out. Another scout went in to get his jacket. To this day it bothers him to be in confined spaces—a feeling I understand well because of my claustrophobia. I don't think he did much caving after that. My private duty patients would often hire Mark to stay with them overnight. He spent many nights in those huge old mansions. He told me that in order to keep awake, he'd walk around the large rooms and along the corridors studying the architecture, oil paintings and antiques in the houses.

You'd think your kid would be safe at the nearby Lutheran church. Ron was playing with some friends and riding an electric go-cart in the church parking lot. Somehow he ended up driving into a pond on the property. His friends carried him back home and laid him on the grass. He was unconscious. My neighbor started to call an ambulance, but I was able to revive him before the call went through.

Another time Ron was canoeing with a bunch of friends on the St. Croix River. The canoe tipped over and Ron went into the water. His friends were busy getting themselves to shore and taking care of the canoe. They didn't realize he couldn't fend for himself, and he nearly drowned before they realized he couldn't swim.

I don't know what's worse—being on the scene when something awful is going on or finding out about it afterwards. And if my immediate family wasn't occupying my attention, I had my folks to worry about.

When my parents got older and needed help, we sold their North Dakota farm. Dad would get confused at night and unlock the door. Mother was afraid he would wander outside. A neighbor of theirs had the same problem and froze to death one night. Mom didn't want that to happen to Dad so they came to live with me in St. Paul. Mom brought her furniture, lamps, and china with her, and we fit it all into our house. In the summer they slept on my enclosed porch.

One weekend Mom called out to me in the garden saying that she couldn't find Dad. We looked around the neighborhood and finally discovered him a few blocks away sitting at a neighbor's picnic table. "I'm visiting my daughter," he told them. "I'm waiting for the train to take me home to Towner. You don't mind if I wait here, do you?" We felt he would be safer in a nursing home. My sister Ruth helped with the cost and visited him. I also worked the evening shift at the same home and they discounted my dad's expenses. Every weekend we'd bring him to my house, but he was always willing to go back. Sometimes I'd take the kids to visit for a few hours. He stayed there until his death in 1963.

My mother lived with us for thirteen years. Yes, there was another person to care for, but her presence was very important to me and to my family. I wouldn't have had it any other way. My parents had supported me one hundred percent. It was the least I could do. Besides, she was queen of the kitchen and her help enabled me to work.

Mother died in January 1975 and was buried in North Dakota, but because we couldn't take all the kids and grandkids there, we had a service at the mortuary. I stood up in front of them and, speaking especially to the kids, said, "Grandma's body was worn out and tired, so she had to leave it. Her soul, though, never dies. It goes on and on and on." She was buried next to my father and their parents at Union Cemetery in Towner.

The trip to North Dakota for her burial was through another winter blizzard. All the radio forecasters advised "Stay off the roads." But we drove right on through it. The wind and cold were terrible. We passed dead cows in the fields. My brother John had flown to St. Paul from San Diego and rode with us. He hadn't driven in snow for years, so I did all the driving. We only stopped for gas. I told everyone we'd be OK because I had an angel sitting on my left fender guiding us. We arrived on time for the funeral. My brother said, "My God, I never believed we'd make it." It sounds unreal but the wind was so strong it drove straw through tree trunks.

The pets we had meant extra work, but they always gave us so much in return. The kids had a succession of dogs, but as the kids got older and involved with their activities, we decided not to get another one after our

160

last dog died. Then the family of a patient I cared for offered me a dog and I decided to take it for Ron. I thought it would be good for him to have a dog of his own. I brought it home and eagerly presented it to him. His response was, "Why did you get me a dog? I'm not interested in having a dog." Mark was finishing high school and working. Heidi was busy with her school friends. I was really disappointed and felt bad. Nobody wanted the dog.

Finally Heidi said she'd take care of it. She picked up on the dog's extreme shyness. It had been kept in a cage and didn't like loud noises. She slept out on the porch with the dog for over a week and soothed it, walked it, trained it and taught it to sit. She even taught it to wait with a treat on its nose and not eat it until she gave a signal.

The dog, a border collie mix, turned out to be a female. Heidi named her Kat Ballou. Kat became a big part of the family. She was the dog who accompanied us on our long trip to the West Coast and guarded the Winnebago at night. Kat was the family dog that Ron rescued the night of the house fire. And she returned the favor. One morning I heard Kat barking out in the yard. I thought she was just playing around and didn't pay much attention. But she persisted, so I went out to see what she was barking about. She ran into the woods in back of the house and led me to Ron. I found him on the ground pulling himself along slowly. He had gone out walking earlier that morning, lost his balance, and couldn't get up again. Kat lived with us until she was old and blind. Greg, Heidi's boyfriend and later her husband, said, "I knew Heidi was the one for me because she had a dog named Kat."

Heidi started dating Greg when she was sixteen. He was seventeen. I didn't like him. Later he asked me why.

"You never looked me straight in the eye," I told him.

"I was afraid you'd kill me with your look."

I wanted Heidi to go to college for at least two years before getting married. But Heidi wanted a wedding instead of college so the money I saved for her education went for their wedding. Heidi and Greg married August 9, 1980.

Joe and I had planned to go on a cruise right after the wedding. We had never taken a cruise together. I arranged for someone to stay with Ron while we were gone. Just before the wedding Heidi approached her dad and asked if she and Greg could come along on the cruise. Heidi's godmother and I had made silk flowers and had done all the decorating for the wedding and Joe and I paid for the wedding and reception. Now the newlyweds wanted to go with us on the cruise. Joe's comment was, "Maybe this is the last time we'll be able to do something nice for them." Joe could never say no to anyone. "We can afford it, can't we?" he asked me. I was the one in charge of family finances, but Joe made this decision. "They're joining us. We'll pay for their honeymoon cruise."

Four days after the wedding we took a flight to Miami and boarded a Princess Line cruise ship. Everything went fine. The next morning, though, Joe told me, "I don't feel too good."

"Well, just rest," I advised him. "Stay on board and take some Dramamine. Maybe you're feeling seasick."

The ship had stopped for the day at Nassau. Our group went to Paradise Island to swim. We were on the beach having a great time when I heard someone calling my name. A motor boat had come to pick up Heidi, Greg and me to take us back to the ship.

Joe was having difficulty breathing, so they had taken him to the hospital in Nassau. I arranged to leave the ship. I had to get packed. Up to that point I had been running around barefoot in a wet, sandy bathing suit. Heidi and Greg continued on with the cruise and I took a taxi to the hospital.

At the hospital Joe was on oxygen. I got Joe settled and signed for everything. They were taking good care of him. As I kissed him good night, I wished it were me in that bed. I had no place to stay. It was already dark and I had to fend for myself. I had stopped at Nassau before with my traveling friend Dorothy, so I knew of the Queen Victoria Hotel. At the nurses' station they got a taxi for me and the two big suitcases we had brought. The taxi was a large truck with a burly driver. It seems we drove through a dark forest to get to the hotel. Once there I never even asked how much the room was. I just unpacked and settled in. I found Joe's flask of whiskey and filled the tub with hot water. The sand had scraped my skin raw.

After a good soaking, I got dressed. I hadn't eaten and the hotel kitchen was closed. Finally someone let me out the kitchen door and told me, "Go down the alley, just keep going. There's a McDonald's a few blocks away." I picked up some food, but when I got back, the kitchen door was locked. I had to go around to the front door and ring the emergency button.

The next day I found out the room cost $150 a night so I switched to a bed and breakfast closer to the hospital. I also found a busboy with a moped and gave him a dollar each time he took me to the beach or wherever I needed to go.

Joe continued recuperating in the hospital. Meanwhile, I had a great time at Nassau. I met a lot of interesting people. Ships came in from China, Africa and other exotic places. I decided I'd just as soon die without any money. From the Chinese ship I bought a jade chess set. Its pieces fit into an elegant case. I had it appraised—it was worth the $350 I paid. I almost bought an aquamarine ring with diamonds that the folks at the store let me wear around for a day. They trusted me to come back! Luckily I've done a lot of traveling and knew how to get around. I relied on my old creed: Whatever will be, will be. I don't worry about things. That's how I manage. I am a total fatalist that way. I had sent messages to Heidi and Greg on the ship, but they didn't get any of them. They didn't know if we were dead, alive or thrown into the creek! Joe was released from the hospital and we flew to Miami then back to Minnesota.

Heidi and Greg lived in Roseville, not far from us, and they both worked until their first child, Jessica, was born four years after they were married. They moved to Stanton, Minnesota, next to a small airfield where we could see skydivers right from their house. "Free as a bird!" I'd say sitting outside on the lawn watching the parachutists drop through the sky.

One of Joe's major house projects was finishing the basement. With wood paneling, a fireplace, bar and extra bathroom, it served us as a place to entertain. Mark claimed it as his space during in his teen years. When he graduated from college and started working, he moved to Heidi's basement where he lived and paid rent. I remember telling him that was a waste of money. I advised him to buy a house. So he bought a house and moved out of the basement. Well, he was in the house with I don't know how many others living there with him. That went sour. He went back to Heidi's basement. That's when he started dating Charlotte. Heidi told me about her. She said, "Well, Mom, don't worry about meeting Charlotte. You won't like her anyway."

"How do you know?"

"You don't think anyone is good enough for Mark."

"You're right," I agreed.

As I've said, Mark always knew his own mind and had very definite ideas about what he wanted to do. Mark took a fulltime job with the local electric utility company, Northern States Power, and started work at their largest coal-burning plant in Becker, Minnesota. He quickly became the youngest plant manager in the company's history. He bought a house in the area and married Charlotte in 1988. She works for the government in the health sector and they have a son named Max. Mark enjoys spending time with Max in nature and showing him animal tracks and plants in the woods. They go pheasant hunting and hunt deer with bow and arrow. When they bring home a deer, Mark makes tasty sausage from the meat.

Mark became very passionate about supporting the threatened peregrine falcons. At the power plant where he worked they put a nesting box on the stack for the birds. The nest even had a camera trained on it so people could watch the chicks as they grew and learned to fly. Soon nests were set up at other power plants. Mark began a program to select grade school children to participate in banding and naming the falcons. He'd speak to students and advise teachers as they developed curriculums for the kids. The program, started at Northern States Power (now Xcel Energy), expanded and even spread to other countries and helped remove the peregrine falcon from the endangered species list. He tells me the falcon nests at the power plants can still be viewed on the Internet.

The Xcel Bowling Team did not excel. In fact, the company's bowling team was forever in last place. Mark took over the team and used management leadership techniques to motivate the bowlers. They took first place and held it for seven years after that. They were the team everyone hated. Joe loved bowling and he had taught Mark a special bowling ball release technique that helped Mark maintain an average of over 200.

Mark's a busy man. When I complained about not seeing enough of him, he told me to catch him on TV. He was in an ad for the power company.

Greg and Heidi had a dog named Frosty, a small Samoyed. He was an all-white puffball when they got him. Unfortunately, Frosty was hit by a car and suffered a hip injury. Jessica was old enough to know not to pull on him, but when their son Josh was born in 1993 and started walking, he'd reach out to Frosty for support. Heidi was afraid that Frosty might bite Josh because of the sore hip so she gave Frosty to me. At eighty I wasn't sure I wanted another animal. By then the backyard was filled with the graves of all our pets. But Frosty was a very special dog. We became inseparable. We'd go out for walks several times a day. He became my excuse to get out and meet the neighbors. Frosty was my great companion for years until he could no longer walk. He died at seventeen.

When the kids were young, I always told them stories at bedtime or to pass the time when we were traveling. Joe asked me, "Why don't you read them stories out of a book?"

"Because this way I can close my eyes. If I read, I'd have to keep my eyes open." I'd also tell stories to the children I took care of as a nurse.

My main character was Oscar the Rabbit who lived in my backyard. I made up all sorts of adventures about him. One story went like this.

Oscar had a skunk friend named Henry, but the other animals wouldn't play with a skunk. He stood out with his white stripe. So Oscar had an idea. "Henry, we'll paint your white stripe black." Soon Henry was playing and dancing together with all the animals, but then it started to rain and the black paint on Henry's white stripe ran off. The other animals were shocked that they had been playing happily with a skunk. "Well," said Oscar, "most of you only believe what you can see. It's very easy to fool you with a bit of paint."

Heidi's children liked my stories. She and Greg had moved to Illinois when Jessica was five years old, and they had Josh and Rachael later. Once they moved, I'd only see them on visits. "Grandma has to tell us stories," they'd say to Heidi. That meant Grandma had to sleep with them. Rachel has a pink canopy bed that makes into two beds. Josh put an air mattress on the floor. I settled in with them and told them stories every single night. "Grandma, what's Oscar doing now? Does he still play with Henry?"

"I could tell them those stories, I've heard them so often," Heidi told me. "But the kids didn't want to hear my Oscar stories, only yours."

℘ 25 ℘

Joe

Joe was raised in St. Gallen, Switzerland, and was twelve years old when he arrived in the United States with his mother and brothers on June 5, 1921. They went to North Dakota and Joe began farming where other relatives had settled. Later he moved to the East and learned coppersmithing. He worked at the top of his trade as a piping specialist. Joe's engineering talents were put to use during World War II dismantling old ships in such a way that the metal could be used to build other ships. His creative side found expression in the candlesticks, vases, plates and other copper objects he made. I displayed his beautiful handiwork on the shelves he built in our kitchen that he remodeled and paneled.

Even though Joe only went to school up to eighth grade in Europe, he could add three figures across, six sets of numbers down and tell you the answer. He was like a calculator. When I did our accounts, I'd read him the figures and he'd tell me the total. Mark has inherited the same ability.

Redoing and maintaining our old farmhouse gave Joe plenty to do. Not only was he good at building and remodeling, but he could also fix anything and that included his '42 Dodge and the '52 Chevy Deluxe that my parents brought from North Dakota when they moved to

Minnesota. He also taught Mark his skills and had him working on cars and fixing things up around the house ever since he was twelve.

Joe and I were a good match. Not only did our work schedules blend, but our tastes, talents and sense of fun were complementary. My preferred instrument was an organ that I bought and taught myself to play while Joe was an accomplished accordionist. He played the harmonica as well. When he and I were on a group tour to Hawaii, we attended an elaborate luau at our hotel in Waikiki. I was standing around in my Hawaiian dress talking to folks when the Hawaiian musicians started playing up on the stage. Suddenly I couldn't believe my ears. Joe was on stage playing "You Are My Sunshine." Next he played "On Top of Old Smokey" and then some German songs. A number of people in our group were of German descent and they were singing along with him. He was so popular that I was sure they were going to offer him a job at the hotel.

Joe and I met at a dance club and we continued dancing our whole lives. We loved ballroom dancing and joined a Western group. For those dances we wore our Western outfits with boots, hats and shirts—the works. We won several dance trophies. We were also regulars at program dances held at the Moose Lodge in St. Paul and at the Masonic Hall in Minneapolis. Evenings began with a supper party at a member's home then we would go to the dance. We filled in our partners' names on dance cards. I truly enjoyed getting dressed up in a formal gown, jewelry and a special hair-do to spend the evening dancing to band music with Joe and our friends. For me, this escape into good fun with friends was the best antidote to the worries and responsibilities of nursing and raising my family.

With the dining and dancing, though, there was also drinking. I can take alcohol or leave it. But Joe struggled with alcoholism. It took me a while to realize this was a problem for him. I'd have two drinks and in the same time span Joe would have three or four and still be totally sober. That should have tipped me off. He had a high tolerance for alcohol. I was never the kind to enjoy visiting and drinking. But that's what he liked to do. He had friends that he'd sit and chat with—and drink. I always had the idea that anyone over eighteen should be responsible for themselves. Joe was always a good man and never became abusive, but he did enter rehab many times as he tried to win this battle. Thank heavens for the insurance from his job at 3M.

I often look back and wonder—was it really me that traveled all that distance? I've had a variegated life, as I call it. A lot has happened. Julie, my good friend from nursing school, was the only one I would talk to about really personal matters. I'd call her when I was at my wit's end. She had a listening ear for me. She'd calmly say, "You never know. Maybe tomorrow will be better, but it could be even worse." Never once did she say, "Oh, that's so terrible, but everything will turn out OK." She and I had a very basic practical understanding about life. I never even told my parents about Joe's drinking problems.

I had married Joe. He was the father of two of my children and he had always taken care of Ron. I wanted the children to be proud of him. I never talked negatively about him to them. They were aware of his drinking problems. I'd tell them, "Your father is someone who has a disease. Some people die from it. Some get cured. Some don't. He probably won't be totally cured. I'm a nurse and I understand it. Believe what I tell you. Kids, love him for the time he's here." Today the children have very fond memories of their dad. Bad things happened but I never let them know. I figured it was my problem and that was that. Good things were mixed up with the bad. Now that they are older, they recall the positive things. They remember how Joe played the harmonica and accordion for them, all the things he taught them, and the fun things he did with them.

No, I was never a victim. I always felt like the glue that held it all together. I did my job.

Eventually Joe had to be cared for in a nursing home. Why couldn't I have taken care of him? Well, I did. Many times. But towards the end, I was still working and dealing with Ron and I couldn't give Joe the medical care he needed at home. After a long last illness, Joe passed away in 1989 at age eighty. He died on August 6, the birthday of his grand-daughter by his first marriage, Carol Ann Violett, Joannie's daughter, and just days shy of Heidi and Greg's August 9 wedding anniversary.

I said to Joannie, "You know I managed your father."

"Yes," she said, "but you did a nice job of it."

After Joe's funeral, Heidi took the kids to the cemetery to see where Joe is buried. Jessica, Josh and Rachel wanted to see their grandfather's grave. Heidi hadn't explained to them that he had been cremated. When they got there, they walked around and saw Joe's name and dates engraved on the stone. Josh looked puzzled. "How could a whole person fit into that tiny space?" he asked and went around the back again. When he reappeared, he announced, "I know what you did. You shrank Grandpa."

Marrying Joe was definitely one of my better life choices.

෨ 26 ෨

Inner Source

"Mom, how do you figure that you have a direct line to God?" Heidi asked me a few years ago. "Nobody else beeps in? You've got it all settled?"

Ever since I was young, I talked to God. I talked about the people in my life, the things that happened. It was my way and I still do it today. I say the same prayers. They aren't fixed prayers like "Now I lay me down to sleep." It's like lifting a telephone receiver and talking direct. It's strictly my way. I pray for other people and hope God remembers them. I believe in a divine power. Yes I do.

Catholics have all these saints. I would never go that route. I always figured if you want anything done, go straight to the head, not through a bunch of other people. And I'm comfortable with that. I have yet to ask God for a privilege or favor. I thank God. These days I'm asking God, "Why are you having me stick around so long?"

I attended church—Lutheran church—when it was convenient. I was often working on Sundays. Religion to me never meant sitting in a pew in church. I don't believe you need a church, but I do go because it helps a lot of people. There was a long period of time when I was traveling that I didn't get to church, but I always said my prayers and talked to God. I know I'm not in any of the categories of religious-type people, but I'm happy and comfortable.

What I think it all comes down to is this: You must properly care for your soul—your inner source. A soul is eternal. The body dies. I've always felt that way. The first thing you are is your inner source, how you yourself are.

I had many opportunities to reflect on life starting when my sister Edna Karin died. Time spent sitting alone in my tree house, watching the cows as they grazed, or riding my horse across the fields lent itself to deep thoughts. My brushes with death made me reflect on how I was living my life. Working as a nurse also gave me plenty to ponder. Long nights spent attending private duty patients and the conversations I had with them all contributed to forming my philosophy of life.

My experiences and reflections have led me to understand that in this universe there is an indescribable force that is the Source. And we each have an inner source. A component of that inner source is intuition which enables us to live and function in this material world. It also guides us to live in harmony with our inner source. Being in harmony with your inner source makes all things happen. If you look far enough and deep enough, you'll find that source. Once you find it, be sure to keep it pure and not dirty it up. Don't lose the connection. Look inside then do your very best. That's a good guideline for each and every day.

My cousin Florence and I grew up together in Towner. Whenever I'd do something outlandish, she'd say, "You are the only one of the whole bunch of us who does different things. Oh well, you've always been fun."

I suppose I could blame my actions on my inner source!

For some reason or other, I have always been very happy with me. My mistakes, my problems don't matter. I still love me. I have a great time with me. I think I'm interesting, fascinating, gorgeous. Sure, my looks have gone. But if no one else likes me, that's okay, because I still do.

I often felt I could sit on a desert island and not be alone. I don't look for adulation. I feel complete. I don't know if that's very logical, but I've never felt that I needed all kinds of things around me. I find enough joy in myself. Or is that just total conceit? I'm not too sure.

One of my friends told me, "You're a great person, but I think you have an over-abundance of self-love." Fine. That just means no one else has to do it.

I know it sounds completely odd, but one of my favorite places for thinking and reflecting as well as relaxing is in my Jacuzzi. I got it through a League of Women Voters raffle. I entered and sure enough they called me to say I had won. To get it I had to borrow a trailer, go to the factory, pick it up and then install it. I wasn't sure what Joe would think about a Jacuzzi so I hired a plumber to put it in. It's the size of a regular bathtub. I loved it right from the start. I settle into the warm churning water and let go of my worries. I just relax and let my mind drift or use the time to reflect and think things through.

I've always been aware that people are created equal. In my mind, other people are as good as I am, but God has yet to make one better. It's a feeling of total equality that has always been a part of how I live.

Others have said things to me and about me that were meant to be critical or hurtful, but my parents taught me early on that "sticks and stones may break my bones but names will never hurt me." To this day that is the creed I follow. I don't let negative stuff from others get to me. They should save their breath.

I don't judge people, and I believe whatever faults others might have can't be solved by harsh or unkind words or deeds. I never go out of my way to make enemies and I can honestly say that I have never intentionally hurt anyone. I taught my children that you've lived a good day if you've never intentionally hurt someone by word or deed. I told them to always try to think three times before saying anything.

Although I never consciously hurt anyone, I do recognize that those who have been the brunt of my jokes might not have enjoyed my sense of humor!

When I look back over my life, I have to wonder at all the heavy-duty decisions I made on my own. I never had anyone to truly depend on to share those responsibilities and decisions with. I could ask Stan, my lawyer friend, about anything and he would tell me his opinion and advise me. He was about my only mentor. I had no one else whose wisdom I trusted. I usually relied on my own intelligence and intuition and rarely asked others for their opinions. Part of the reason was that I was deeply aware of the need to be true to myself.

To remain true to oneself is a fulltime job that never ends. We are born with a clean slate on which we draw our very own pictures for life. Whatever you do stays with you the rest of your days along with early impressions even though they are often camouflaged by the very act of living.

All my thinking and reflecting and developing a philosophy of life has nourished and supported me. It's funny how I don't seem to need it when I'm having a good time and things are going smoothly! But when life gets rough, it's what sustains me. It's like having a set of wings that lets me fly above my troubles to get a perspective on them. It's been a great resource.

If I had had a different mind set, I'm not sure I would have survived with Ron. Raising and caring for him pushed me beyond myself and played a big part in developing my inner resources and finding my inner source.

Yet I don't stay awake at night worrying about things. I just turn my mind off like a switch. I wasn't always this way. I had to develop that mentality in order to face situations I truly couldn't change. I treated them as lightly as possible, did the best I could and moved on.

I'm a concrete sort of person. To me it's a basic fact of life that whatever will be, will be. Perhaps I miss a lot of emotions that others have by being that way, but I'm not callous. At least I don't think I am. I have this belief that nothing is ever going to knock me down. They haven't made anything in this world that I'm afraid of—not people or anything.

It's interesting to look back and see how my life experiences have shaped my beliefs and how, in turn, my beliefs have shaped my life. Developing a philosophy for one's own life is a truly exciting and rewarding endeavor. To me it's like having a garden to tend, shape and watch grow. And like a garden, it's always there even when I'm not tending it.

I take all sorts of actions and do things, yet I always believe that God will provide. I told one of my pastors that I have this sense that God will take care of me. It's a feeling of complete faith. It may not seem like it should really work in this world, yet that's how I feel. Whether in daily life or facing a major decision or a difficult situation, I knew God would take care of things. Yet I also worked plenty hard. In the background of my mind was the thought: What will be, will be. The future's not mine to see. I feel sorry for people who fuss and fume and get themselves all nervous and excited—for what!

This ability I have to accept that what will be, will be is, I think, one of the reasons I've lived so long. One of my friends said, "That's why you don't have gray hair. You don't worry."

When people heard about my skydiving, they'd ask me, "Aren't you concerned about the chute opening?"

"Absolutely not," I'd say. "If it's supposed to open it will."

To escape worrying I simply close my eyes and don't think about anything. I just blank everything out. I get a feeling like when I jump out of an airplane—a feeling of space, nothing in particular.

When problems come up, I'd think "I'm supposed to be worried about this." But I just let it go by. I shut out what I don't like. Blank it out.

If I can't do something to change a situation, I just let it go. My mother worried. When she got over one worry, I'd tell her, "Mother, quick, you have to find another worry." Worrying just uses up all the good energy!

As people get older, they fuss about this, are concerned about that. I suppose it's a sign of intelligence. Others can fret about things, but I don't. I just get up and live each day. I don't know if I'll be here tomorrow. Maybe it's a stupid way to live, but it keeps you from having furrows and wrinkles. Even when things weren't going well, I felt that way. Ron is a worry wart. He worries if his aides will come, if too much money is being spent. He worries about what's going to happen.

My husband Joe would fume and brood about things. I'd tell him, "One hundred years from now you won't know the difference." That made him mad.

I also notice that a lot of people dwell on the past. If they can't find something to worry about in the present, they worry about the past! They say they wish they had done this or not done that. As far as I'm concerned, what's done is done. I let others resurrect the bad things. I don't do that.

I truly believe that my whole life is already written in The Book. It's never a great surprise what happens. I'm not concerned about what will or will not work out. When you do that, you are more carefree. I have a carefree attitude. I let others do the worrying.

When my kids would dispute me, I'd say, "Don't argue with me. It's all in The Book."

"Where's The Book?" they'd ask.

"You'll never know."

The Lord made me tough. My life must have been the reason. But as my mother told me, "The Lord only gives you exactly what you can bear." In my prayers at night I say, "Thanks, Lord. You can have my troubles. I'm going to sleep."

I certainly don't feel sorry for me. I feel I deserve all the good things I get—and then some.

❧ 27 ☙

Golf, Garden, and Glory

I started playing golf at age forty. That's fifty-three years of putting around. I began playing as a way to socialize and meet people—men. Then it became a chance to spend time outdoors and be with others. I've played golf with the same team of women for twenty-six years. Isn't that wild? We always met over at Red Lobster and exchanged fun gifts every year. I've played golf with one woman in the group for forty years. We traveled to Florida every winter to get in some rounds under the sun. I also play with my son Mark. We played a game last summer for my ninety-third birthday. I won't tell who won.

Golf was always just a fun activity for me. My garden, though, is my support and refuge. I followed my mother's example. She was a tremendous gardener who planted by the moon. That's called "biodynamic gardening." Dynamic is right. She earned her pin money from her flowers. She made wreaths and bouquets to sell. She could make anything grow even in North Dakota. And it was all organic. She never used store-bought fertilizer in her garden.

Joe and I planted our garden each spring. We grew our own vegetables and ate from the garden over the summer. When the watermelons were getting ripe, Mark would set up his pup tent by the watermelon patch and spend the night watching them. He didn't trust the neighbors.

The backyard was huge. It reminded me of waving wheat fields in North Dakota. Before we started working on it, it was just tall weeds and patches of gravel. When the kids were growing up, we had badminton courts, baseball diamonds and vinyl swimming pools. Joe and I worked full time and we didn't have a lot of time to do yard work, so the process of shaping that expanse into the garden it is today took many years. I had to cut the grass down and cultivate plants in certain areas. I dug out the rest. A friend gave me some ferns. Someone else gave me daylilies and phlox and other cuttings. I just kept at it. I bought a sit-down Toro mower with two disposal buckets to mow the lawn. It was expensive but worth it. I couldn't work without it. Another tool I'd never be without is my own chainsaw!

Many times my garden was my salvation. I knew it and I used it. It was my answer for everything, especially situations I knew I couldn't change or fix. I'd often be deeply upset about something that had happened at work or with Ron or someone else in the family and I'd go into the garden and start working. That way I didn't get angry or depressed. I just dug in the dirt. It calmed me and put me back together somehow. It's very healing for me to work in the yard. I require that type of activity. Besides, there's always something that needs to be done out there. If I ever became too disabled to get into my garden and work, I think I would probably die.

The back door of the house used to open onto a flagstone patio where we had the barbecue and sometimes put up a canopy tent. Now I have a three-season porch that allows me to enjoy my garden. We built it as an addition in the 1980s. I've never enjoyed any part of my house as much.

What comes in a close second is the veranda—my fancy name for the front porch that I had reconstructed a few years ago because it was collapsing. It used to be enclosed and we used it for sleeping in the summer and for storage the rest of the time. When I had it repaired, I restored it as a traditional porch with lots of places to sit. I even bought a bistro table and chair set.

When I want company, I turn on the front lights and neighbors come over with their own drinks. We have impromptu parties and get-togethers on my veranda all throughout the Minnesota summer and as far into the fall as we can. That's what porches are for. Years ago before air conditioning, in the older sections of town, people sat on their porches, especially in the evenings, to catch the cool breezes, entertain, watch the neighbors, and greet one another.

It's the best therapy. It's porch therapy. There's nothing like having a group of friends around to laugh and be with especially when life gets bumpy. At my porch soirees, we never run out of things to talk about. We do a good job entertaining ourselves and caring about each other.

But back to my three-season porch. From here I can watch hummingbirds sip nectar from the orange honeysuckle vine. I see that my bird feeders are a popular hang out. Butterflies hover around my flowers. The bright yellow black-eyed susans really stand out next to the white phlox. Chipmunks scamper around. Here is where I observe Oscar the Bunny and his activities and get material for my stories. He comes up to the screen door when he wants to tell me something or to listen to me.

Although my screened porch is a utilitarian space with green outdoor carpeting, it's a magical space for me. Now the hummingbird is checking out the giant butterflies hanging on the windows. Here are all the things I like—many of them gifts from friends—chimes, birdhouses, stained glass hangings, a carved wooden parrot. I'm nourished by the lush green around me, the bright geraniums and perky impatiens, lilies, pansies, and soft breezes. Nice life.

I had to have a parrot on the porch. Parrots are one of my favorite creatures. My first introduction to them was at a neighbor's when I was

179

growing up in North Dakota. They had a small clever parrot. I almost got a parrot when Ron was little but opted for Petey the parakeet instead. On a trip to Cancun with Heidi, I spotted a large bronze and copper parrot. I knew I wanted it but they were asking more than I was willing to pay. Besides, I hadn't brought any cash with me because, as I told Heidi, there was nothing I really needed. "Come on, Heidi," I said, heading out the door, "we have to get out of here!"

"But Mom, you really liked it. When you see something that spectacular, it's worth it." She insisted we go back in. Heidi made an offer and the shopkeeper accepted. She had just enough cash to buy it for me. I walked out with the huge metal parrot. We laugh about this every time she comes and sees the parrot hanging in the corner of my kitchen!

My parrot obsession didn't stop there. I took a stained glass workshop and made a small hanging with a bird. My wonderful instructor Patty created an entire stained glass window for me out of imported Danish glass from my design. It's a parrot, of course. Then there are my crazy parrot string lights on the veranda. I always liked parrots because they are so colorful and loud, long-lived and intelligent.

I've always been curious about everything and everyone. Whatever I did was an opportunity to learn so I was never bored. For me that's a key to living well—an active mind. I found lots of things to do and learn.

With my family, nursing, the house and garden, golfing and travel, I didn't have much time to sew, but I love textiles. My large collection of clothes gives evidence of that! On my last trip to Switzerland with Joe we bought cuckoo clocks for everyone which I stuffed with skeins of beautiful Swiss yarn for the return trip. At home I knitted a coat from the yarn and lined it. The coat won a blue ribbon at the Minnesota State Fair. I also knitted a prize-winning jacket using several strands of yarn together. My grandmother who raised canaries started teaching me to sew when I was eight. She even taught me how to make bias tape.

I took a class to learn how to weave wall hangings. What fascinated me about those textiles is that from the back the piece looks like a confusing mess, but the front is a beautiful work of art. Sort of like life, I think.

My friend Julie and I learned to upholster chairs. We both were proud of all the chairs we re-covered and the money we saved by doing it ourselves.

When we weren't covering chairs, we played bridge together. We had a bridge group made up of our nursing school friends that met for many years. Our group of nurses lived long lives! We were social players, more interested in conversation than winning.

Having the bridge group over meant making desserts. Julie always aimed for an oooh-and-ahhh dessert each time she entertained. Because I was usually working, I tended to serve easy treats. But I love to bake traditional Norwegian stollen bread made with cardamom to give it that unique Scandinavian taste.

Besides baking when I had time, I tried other crafts like collage and calligraphy. I remember writing with my special pen: "I may not be perfect but parts of me are excellent!" Given my love of talk, Toastmasters was a natural for me. I never have any trouble coming up with a speech. I just open my mouth and listen to what comes out!

On a recent visit to Heidi's house in Illinois, she didn't want me to drive. They live out a ways and I felt like a one-legged horse not being able to get around on my own. Her husband Greg asked me if I wanted to go into town with him.

"Yes, because I'm making dinner and want to pick out my own meat." What I really wanted to do was to stop at a clothing store where I had seen some tops I liked in the window. What can I say? I adore clothes. I think it's funny that a kid who would never wear anything feminine ends up as a clotheshorse. Maybe I love having clothes so much because when I was roaming the West Coast what didn't fit into my one suitcase I gave away, so I ended up with very few clothes.

I like clothes and putting together outfits, but I'm not obsessed by anything. Neurosis about money or personal belongings is a hard thing for me to comprehend. We're not going to take anything with us. Whatever will be, will be. I find it hard to understand people who indulge their anxieties. My neighbor across the street taught me how to enjoy cognac in front of the fireplace discussing politics and current affairs. But I don't have to take these problems into my life. I'm able to close my eyes after saying my prayers and fall asleep.

Once at Heidi's house, I was sitting alone in the living room with my eyes closed. My two grandkids came in and watched me for a while. Then they walked over to me and opened my eyes. "Grandma, what are you doing?" they asked.

"I'm smoothing my soul," I told them. It's my version of Tai Chi. I take the time to quiet my mind and untangle my feelings. I do this regularly. I smooth my soul and get myself back to a calm space inside.

So where's the glory in my life? Yes, I've gotten recognition, bits of fame and attention. But the real glory is in being at peace within, being in touch with the inner source. Then add to that having fun with people, helping others and engaging deeply with them. Great fun is high on my list of priorities. Creating is great fun—whether it's a place for flowers to grow and birds to come, or food to share and enjoy, wall hangings, a stunning outfit or a beautiful room. Strong ties with friends and family are definitely part of glory. And it's not just the easy, satisfying and fun parts, but the heart-stopping events, the challenges that drive you deeper into your soul. All this goes into real glory.

I did go out and grab some glory by skydiving. That wasn't just a whim. I thought it out carefully and planned my venture to make a point—and have some great fun!

❧ 28 ☙

Skydiving Fame

What makes you do things like that? My relatives in Alabama asked me this when I sent them a tape of my skydive.

I think more people would do adventurous and interesting things if they could find the time. But if you clutter yourself up with fear and worries about money, appearances and all that, there isn't enough time for things that have more meaning.

People ask me, "Aren't you afraid to jump out?" I've lived longer than most. My attitude is, "So what! Jumping out of an airplane is no big deal."

Before I jump, even while I'm getting hooked up and sitting on Kerry's lap, all I'm thinking is free, free. I'm pressed on all sides by the other jumpers crowded into the plane, but being free is my escape from feeling compressed, physically or mentally. Then we stand up and take two steps to the door. I'm thoroughly attached to another person, but I tell myself: Think free. Free. You can do a lot with how you think. It all depends on your state of mind. Jumping out wasn't of great concern to me. But I understand that for others, it might be.

Of course, I'm not dumb or naïve. I consider myself quite realistic. I'm told that no one has ever died tandem jumping, but still, you sign your life away. And you pack your own chute. In each one, there's an emergency chute so, if for some reason the tandem jumper can't pull the release, the emergency chute will open automatically. If circumstances were different and I were much younger, I'm sure I'd try solo jumping. I was very interested in getting silver wings for jumping. In the military you earn silver wings after five jumps. I figured, given my life and character, they'll probably be the only wings I'll ever get.

Then there's the question of fame and negotiating the price of publicity. I did achieve my goals—to shake things up and draw attention to what folks can do even at age ninety. I had fun. I loved being in New York with my daughter Heidi and appearing on *The CBS Early Show*.

Hannah Storm asked me about doing a better job than senior Bush who landed on his tail when he jumped at eighty. I told her, "Women are a little more graceful, don't you think?"

I said that I had wanted to leave something special to my grandkids. "This is one grandmother they aren't going to forget!"

I never considered age a big deal. It always bugs me when people ask me how old I am. For me, it's what's inside that counts and being young at heart. But once I declared my age, I had to face the fact of being ninety. I had lied on my driver's license. I even took four years off my birth date that was chiseled in stone at the cemetery where Joe is buried. My little lie lost me the chance to appear on *The Tonight Show* with Jay Leno. They checked Minnesota drivers license records and said I wasn't really ninety.

I never told people my age. When someone asked me how old I was, I'd say "You've confided things to me. A woman who tells her age will reveal anything. You wouldn't want me to tell the things you've said to me in confidence, would you?"

Because I ignored my years, I never felt the weight of being ninety. Accepting the age I am was hard because we have all these ideas of what that age is "supposed" to be.

Princess Diana's biographer, Andrew Morton, was in the Green Room before his appearance on *The Early Show* that morning to present his new book *Diana: In Pursuit of Love*. "You're not really ninety, are you?" he asked. "You can't be ninety. You don't have gray hair and wrinkles all over. You're lively and fun!"

Like I said to my son's dentist back in St. Paul, "You can't tell anything by appearances. You can't tell by the looks of a frog how far it can jump." He couldn't believe I had actually skydived. "Not you," he said. "You are too tiny, too petite, too fragile."

After my TV appearance, I was curious about all the fuss and publicity, and I wondered why an old lady popping out of an airplane was so exciting to people. Later that summer I went to see my fifty-year-old dermatologist. "Oh, you're the lady who jumped out of the plane. I've never shaken the hand of a celebrity. Let me shake your hand. You know, I'm not a fearful person, but I don't think I could do it."

I hope my jump gave wings to the idea that you are never too old to do something exciting. Actual numbers don't mean that much. It's what you yourself are. Or maybe I just haven't grown up yet.

But I did have a lot of fun. During our stay in Manhattan, we walked from our hotel to Times Square. I wanted to eat someplace where I knew what I was eating, so we went to an Italian place. The manager came over to me. "I saw you on TV. You were great! Here, I have the best table for you. Now order a special dessert," he urged me later. "I think you should be a little heavier." When we asked for the check he said, "No check. It's a pleasure to have you as my guest." How about that for being treated royally in New York!

We walked into Saks Fifth Avenue and a woman came over and asked to shake my hand. "I think you're the greatest," she said. We also took in a Broadway play, *The Producers*. I could really get used to this!

The following Christmas I spent with Heidi in Illinois. It was non-stop activity that included a soak in a hot tub and dining out. Heidi and I were shopping and decided to stop at a restaurant for lunch and a drink. It was busy and we ended up sitting at the bar and talking. After a while the guy we were seated next to introduced himself. He said he'd been depressed and out of sorts but then he overheard us. "You made my day," he told me. He said he would contact the local TV station, and sure enough the next day I was interviewed at Heidi's house and was on TV again! He also invited us to his own restaurant, the Moon River Supper Club, where he introduced me to his partner and treated us to a wonderful dinner.

My granddaughter Rachel made a book with her mom's help that tells about my skydiving. "Now the kids believe me when I tell them about my grandma skydiving," she told me. "They used to say, 'Grandmothers don't do that.'"

After my first skydive, I wanted to experience a longer free fall so we could do more things while freefalling. I asked Kerry how fast we dropped. He said that with our combined weights, we traveled at 120 miles an hour before our parachute opened. One of my jumps that summer was cancelled because President Bush was in town, but by my next birthday I got my wings. Heidi and her friend jumped with me for my fifth jump on my birthday. That was the nicest birthday present in the world.

Kerry arranged a big surprise for me. He contacted the U.S. Parachute Association and the regional director authorized a special set of gold wings for me. Gold wings are for skydivers who make 1,000 jumps, so these are very special. I also qualified to join Skydivers Over Sixty.

Heidi and I were flown to New York again and I was interviewed by Renae Stiler on *The CBS Early Show*. She introduced me saying I'd turned into an "adrenalin junkie."

"What do you get out of it?" she asked me.

"It's an adrenalin high. I don't smoke pot or anything, but I think I get a zing out of it. Right after you leave the plane there's this wonderful period of weightlessness when you can do all sorts of things."

"What does it feel like taking the jump out the door of the airplane?"

"I just go with it," I said. On my last dive, Heidi's parachute came close to mine. There was my very own daughter sailing through the sky with me! That was something beautiful.

I also told Renae that even at my age—I was ninety-one then—it's not the end. It's just the beginning.

After my TV appearance we ate, walked through Saks and Bergdorf Goodman's, then went on a carriage ride through Central Park. Heidi asked me what else I would like to do. "See another Broadway show," I said. We saw *Dirty Rotten Scoundrels*. I liked the staging.

Harry Smith came by while I was at CBS. "I had to see you again even though I just got back from a safari to Africa."

That was so sweet. "Here comes my boy," I said when I saw him.

"Only my mom ever spoke to me that way," he said. "It makes me all soft inside."

We had such a wonderful moment after my first appearance the year before. "What do you feel like?" Harry asked me then.

"I feel so happy I could dance," I told him.

"Why don't we?" And that's what we did. We danced in the studio dodging the cameras and stepping over cables. It was magical!

℘ 29 ℘

Heights and Depths

I'm calling this chapter "From the Heights to the Depths in One Easy Step." I went skydiving twice more the summer of my ninetieth birthday. At least it wasn't raining for my second jump. That meant we could go up to 19,000 feet. This time freefall lasted twelve seconds. I enjoyed being a bird again. I love that feeling of freedom, of belonging up there in the sky. You can see soooo far.

When I wasn't jumping out of airplanes, I was working in my garden. It requires my constant attention. The phlox by the fence are out of control and have to be transplanted to the bare spot in back. The day lilies have proliferated themselves out of space, but they are a pain to dig up. And so it goes. I try to get out golfing whenever I can as well. It's a nice life if you can stand it!

Labor Day a friend invited me out to a sports-themed restaurant with tables and seats like a stadium. That was okay until it came time to leave. The seats required stepping on a rail. When I got up to leave, my foot slipped and down I went with a crack. I had the wind knocked out of me—as well as all the liquids I had accumulated in my bladder. Of course, everyone made a fuss and they called an ambulance.

The absolutely worst part of all this is now everyone recognizes me—the High Flyer down on the floor on her back.

They took x-rays in the emergency room. Nothing was broken so I was sent home with muscle relaxants and pain pills. The pain was really terrible. My back muscles were in constant spasm. All I could really do with any comfort was sleep. It was excruciating to turn over in bed or get up to go to the bathroom. It was a real struggle. Fortunately, I have wonderful family members and neighbors to help. Otherwise it would have been impossible.

Just as I was feeling better, I injured my back again. This time I called my son Mark and he took me to the hospital where they admitted me. Imagine me the nurse now flat on my back in severe pain, totally dependent on other nurses, aides and doctors for everything. Not a pretty sight.

I'm not one to swallow my opinion or hold it in. No one was really asking my opinion on things, but I gave it anyway. In the ER they bounced me around like a sack of potatoes. "I'm not a rubber duckie," I told them as they chucked me onto the gurney, slung me onto the x-ray table, then bounced me back into the Emergency Room bed. This exquisite handling continued my entire stay. How do people who are in really desperate condition survive?

Although I've been around hospitals and people needing care all my life, I hadn't realized how much things have changed. There's no such thing as a bed bath in the hospital anymore. At least not in the hospital I was in. They just hand you a towel and tell you to clean yourself. When I was a practicing nurse, bed baths were an important part of patient care.

By the time I'd been in the hospital a few days, I was pretty annoyed with the ER doctor who saw me the first time I fell. He was so sure of himself and accepted no input from me. He was determined to get this old lady in line. Why should I put up with someone who does-n't listen to me? I didn't want to see him any more. I asked to have another doctor assigned to me. Of course, the ER doctor showed up in my room one day. "What are you doing here?" I asked him. "I fired you." He assured me he was just on rotation and checking in on patients. "Well, I'm sure you get along with people much better than I do," I said and I shook his hand.

I had been in the ER twice and in the hospital six days and no one had bothered to check my back for bruises. I had to insist that someone look at it. What a surprise—I had a big, puffy, black and blue mark.

I feel sorry for the meek and mild in that setting. You have to speak up for what you need. But for the most part, it's just like running sheep through a dip before shearing. There's nothing you can do about it. It's the system and it's their way or no way.

When I was in nursing, I used to coach patients about what to ask their doctors to get the information they needed to know. I'd make them learn the important questions to ask.

The medical system is a huge impersonal conglomerate. There's little compassion in it. I had to insist that they take another x-ray. I needed it for my peace of mind. I had fallen a second time, as I reminded them. The x-ray came back negative and I was happy about that. Now I knew it was just a matter of time and of—oh no!—rehab.

For some reason I had to spend four days in rehab at the hospital to learn how to poach an egg and other useful operations. But I decid-ed to go along with the deal. It seems that the point of physical and occupational therapy is to prove you can do things like washing dishes, going to the toilet, walking up steps. "I don't have steps in my house," I told the therapist. She wasn't convinced. "Okay, let's just do it and get it over with," I told her as I zipped up and down her stairs. Then came the resistance weights. I'm a gardener, remember, and that summer I had hauled forty-two wheelbarrows of dirt around my garden. "Hey," I said to the therapist, "you need to work out with these weights. You're not as strong as I am."

I know they were glad to see me leave the hospital. As I told them on discharge, "I'll leave with your good wishes or without." There's a good side to being ancient. You can say it as it is without apologies. Actually, it's a nice stage to be in. I'm enjoying it.

After serving my time in the health care jail, I finally got home. Mark and his wife Charlotte brought me back. Mark is one of the quiet folks. He observes people. He's reserved—not like his mother. Even as a kid I never knew what he was thinking. Charlotte was straightening up my house which I hadn't done a thing to since my first fall at the restaurant when Mark said to me, "I hope you'll be able to manage by yourself."

"I'd tell you if I couldn't," I assured him.

"You know, we'd rest a lot easier if you were in a place were people can take care of you."

"Take care of me? You know me—they'd have me thrown in jail for slander. Or I'd run around without any clothes on just because things were too boring."

I've really been shaking my kids up since my ninetieth birthday. I sometimes wonder if I should let them have some peace.

My family tells me I was the worst patient they ever had in the hospital. Well, I'm glad I get recognition for something!

ဢ 30 ca

The Eyes Have It

Now I know people don't like hearing about a bunch of ailments, but I'm going to tell this story for what you can get out of it. I have had spectacular health for most of my life. No complaints from me in that department—except for my ratty teeth, but I fixed that problem.

Then I developed an eye condition called Fuchs' Syndrome. That meant bad news for my eyes. When a new cornea was put in, the epithelia cells weren't strong enough to support the cornea because my eyes dry out. Aging is the greatest factor in my condition. I was in my eighties when this started. It's genetic in origin. Looking back, I remember all the folks on my father's side had bad eyesight, wore thick glasses, and used magnifying lenses.

But I didn't know this when I went to see the first eye doctor. What a pain he was. I could tell that he thought I was just an old lady and why bother with her. What a disgusting experience. He was terribly professional, right to his fingertips. He wasn't at all concerned about me. "Doctor," I finally said, "I don't think you have any interest in working with older people."

"Oh no," he protested, "I do."

"Well, I feel you don't, so we aren't going to work together any more." I left his office.

It's distressing enough to have something the matter with you, especially your eyes. Add to that a medical professional who doesn't relate to you or hear you, and it feels worse. I had to find another eye doctor and I did. That was Dr. Scott Uttley. I love him! He took the time to talk to me and didn't treat me as just Old Lady Patient X. Besides being nice, he's cute. He said to me, "I never had a grandmother. You are more than a grandmother. You're a friendly grandmother." He showed me pictures of his kids and we got to talking as real humans. He even began using my first name. And I could talk freely about my fears. I told Dr. Uttley, "I'm practicing walking around my house with my eyes shut."

"You're not going to go blind, Aileen," he said, "not if I have anything to do with it!" I felt confidence in him. He understood why I wanted to see as well as possible and he was interested in working with me. He was also interested in skydiving and wanted to see me jump. He gave me his cell and home phone numbers to let him know when I'd be jumping.

He kept his word and treated me. I've had three cornea transplants. It's not that I have three eyes. One had been done wrong previously and was redone by Dr. Uttley. I only had local anesthesia. He asked if I could lie still for two and a half hours without moving. "I'll do it," I said. "You just worry about my eyes."

When they took out the stitches, I could actually read my birthday cards. The doctor says I'm the only person with this syndrome who has recovered eyesight to this degree. He even wrote a paper on my case for a medical conference.

"Are you going to mention my skydiving in your presentation?" I asked him.

"I don't think so, Aileen."

❧ 31 ❧

Let the Good Times Roll

When I jumped out of that plane on my ninetieth birthday, I had no idea what I was leaping into. Or who would leap into my life. In New Orleans a young man was watching TV with his friends. My skydive story and interview came on.

"That's my grandmother!" the young man said.

"No way."

"Yes, that's her. She lives in St. Paul where I was born. That's my grandmother!"

Ron's son, Ronnie Bruce, called and said he had seen my jump on TV and that he was proud of his grandmother. "I always knew you'd do something like that," he said. It was good to hear from him, but we didn't really know too much about him. Long stretches of time went by when we didn't have any news at all. Every now and then Ron would say he had a feeling that things weren't going well for Ronnie Bruce, so I'd call the police where he was living to make sure nothing bad had happened to him. We had no way of getting in touch with him.

It was a battle to maintain contact with Ronnie Bruce when he was little. Ron was granted one weekend a month to visit his son after the divorce. Ronnie Bruce's mother Cindy would bring him over to stay the weekend until he was six, but she married a few more times and moved around. When Ronnie Bruce was thirteen, I took him, Ron, Heidi and her daughter Jessica to Disney World. But then we lost touch with him until we heard he was living in New Orleans. When he contacted me after my jump, I decided to visit him.

In April of 2005 I went to New Orleans with my longtime friend Jan Sandberg and her daughter Terry Dervie. Jan had a business event in Texas and joined us later in New Orleans. Terry flew with me. I couldn't have made the trip without her. She was my chaperone! I decided to work my skydiving granny fame for all it was worth to make sure we had a good trip. On the second leg of the trip, from Houston to New Orleans, we were assigned separate seats in a smaller plane—just the kind that gives me claustrophobia. Oh no! I wanted Terry next to me. "Look," I said to the attendant, "jumping out of a plane at ninety entitles me to sit where I want now." With Terry at my side, I felt better and could distract myself from that awful claustrophobic feeling.

We went right to our hotel in the French Quarter where Ronnie Bruce met us. He and I had several fun days together. I thoroughly enjoyed the New Orleans lifestyle—strolling around the streets, meeting people, talking to folks, joking with strangers, laughing a lot, and stopping in bars and coffee shops to hang out with Ronnie Bruce's friends. I loved the vibrant French Quarter with people everywhere and music at all hours. I had a great time. The best part, of course, was getting to know my grandson.

I think he bears a lot of scars from his upbringing. You have to forgive, if you are a Christian, the omissions caused by the traumas of his life. It was painful for me as his grandmother to hear his story.

"It was tough," he said. "My mom was always on government assistance. The kids at school teased me constantly. So at sixteen I left home. I rode the rails and hung out with other runaways."

"Where did you stay? What did you do for food," I asked, wishing I had known. He could have lived with us.

"Sometimes I lived in the rail yards. I panhandled for food money. I spent some time in New York, wandered all over the country and then ended up in New Orleans. There I met someone who gave me a job and a place to stay."

"Did you know anyone when you went to these places?'

"No," he said. "And I didn't want anyone to know me."

Not a bright situation. But Ronnie Bruce is a good guy. He's a lot like my brother John—soft-spoken, not a catalyst-type person. He's a quiet, gentle individual who thinks things over before speaking. My brother, though, had a real humorous and mischievous side like me.

Ronnie Bruce has a facial tattoo that is light gray-blue like his eyes. "So what's the symbolism?" I asked him.

"Nothing," he said, "I just wanted to do it."

"Well, it's certainly unique." Ronnie Bruce is blond and has a goatee. He's well groomed, tall and slender. At least he looks tall to his petite grandma!

When I offered to send some money to his checking account, he said, "Don't have a checking account, Grandma. Never had one."

"But you have a cell phone."

To me, Ronnie Bruce is an artistic free soul, very intelligent with his own ideas of how he wants to live. He doesn't acquire things. His New Orleans apartment was small and very neat. There was one hanging fern plant. He works just enough to earn the money he needs. He has a part-time job and uses his free time to study. At twenty-eight, he has been in New Orleans for ten years. He's gotten to know artists and craftspeople and has learned glass blowing and painting from them. China interests him and we talked about my trip there. He wants to go China to live.

Jan and Terry joined us for more strolling, a bar stop and visiting. I was so glad I had come. Getting to know Ronnie Bruce and seeing him in his environment was important for me. As we flew back to Minnesota, I began plotting.

196

I take risks. It'll either turn out a total disaster or a great success. I invited Ronnie Bruce to come up to St. Paul for a week in July to see his dad, but I didn't tell Ron because he would have said, "No, no, I'm too sick." I just had Ronnie Bruce walk in to surprise him. "Your heart's in good condition, Ron, so you can't have a heart attack," I said. Ronnie Bruce stayed with his dad. "You have a nice place," he told him. We did something every day. I'm so happy when risks work out.

We looked at the large and stately birch tree we planted in the backyard with Ronnie Bruce many years ago. While we were in the backyard, Ronnie Bruce demonstrated kung fu and broke two two-by-fours. I was impressed! He also did very well on a par three golf course. "Why don't you go into professional golf?" I asked him.

"If I did," he said, "I'd have to worry about money."

"OK, I know you don't worry about money, but I do. How did you get to the airport from New Orleans? It's quite a ways out."

"I've got a friend who lives near the airport. I went to his place, stayed up all night and walked to the airport for the 5 AM flight. But don't worry, Grandma. Another friend who drives a taxi is picking me up."

Ronnie Bruce has never had a credit card and didn't have an ID until he had to get one for the trip. He had to get it with his birth certificate. At least he will never be in debt like so many people today! It seems his idea is to live in the world but not be of it. He has friends who live the same way.

I figured that out when I met his friends in New Orleans like the one who makes jewelry and sells it at fairs. Ronnie Bruce also likes to paint, but glass blowing is his main skill. Before he left St. Paul, I took him to the thrift store where he picked out four shirts of the same style. He dresses very simply.

I'm glad we kept working at bonding with Ronnie Bruce. Now there's some rapport between him and his dad. He never sees his mother. At times I think that her behavior wasn't directed so much at Ron as at me. She knew I understood her and she knew my opinion of her. It's as if she decided to show me that I wasn't going to have everything the way I wanted it. I thought back to those visits we had when Ronnie Bruce was little. When his mom wasn't looking, he'd wave at us.

"Do you remember anything from your childhood?" I asked him.

"Some parts," he said.

"They were not good."

"No, that's true. But I've always depended on myself. I could never depend on my mother. You know, Grandma, even way back then I always knew you were there."

✷ 32 ✷

Katrina Comes Calling

The entire nation was watching as Hurricane Katrina smashed into New Orleans and the southern states. I was horrified at what happened, especially when so much of the death and destruction seemed to be caused by negligence and incompetence. Having visited New Orleans only a few months before, I felt it especially hard. I wondered what was happening to all the people I had met. Ron and I were concerned about Ronnie Bruce.

It was several days before we heard from him, but he called and told us he had driven out of New Orleans before Katrina made landfall. He was safe. That was a relief.

Then he asked me, "Some of my friends don't have any place to go. Can we all come and stay with you?"

I didn't even think twice. "Ronnie Bruce, you are part of my family. I will do what I can to help you and your friends." On the news I was constantly hearing about people going here and there and being offered places to stay by strangers. I thought, Why not? What better thing could I do to help out those affected by Katrina than share my big house? "Sure," I said. "I've got plenty of room. Which friends and how many?"

"How about four—that's two couples."

"Okay. Five in all." I was mentally assigning the rooms in my house and figuring out how to furnish them. "When will you be coming?"

"My friends still have to be rescued out of New Orleans first, and then we have to see how we can get to Minnesota. I'll let you know."

"Well, at least that will give me time to get the house ready."

"Great. By the way, one of the women is pregnant and her baby is due in November."

Fortunately, I have great neighbors and friends and I know who to call at the social service agencies. I knew that the New Orleans refugees would receive government assistance. Meanwhile, I had to spring into action and round up beds, furniture and supplies for my five house guests.

I cleared out my basement and garage. Friends brought over a bed and bedding, lamps, a couch and easy chairs, even a refrigerator. We gathered all sorts of baby things to have ready. I felt like I was running a junior Salvation Army. It meant so much to me to see the generous response. People really helped. They donated personal supplies and brought over food as well. I really wanted Ronnie Bruce and his friends to settle into a welcoming house and have some time to recover from the trauma of the hurricane.

The five arrived after a series of rides that got them to St. Paul. Besides Ronnie Bruce, there were Kristina and Mort who were long-time friends of Ronnie Bruce, and Nathan and Tracy. Tracy had just moved to New Orleans eight months previously from Oregon. Nathan, also a friend of several years, was originally from Ohio. They came with the clothes on their backs and little else. They were able to register with FEMA in St. Paul (the Federal Emergency Management Agency) and apply for benefits. Kristina's baby was due in early November, so she had to find a clinic and a doctor.

Since I live alone in a large house, having five guests worked out quite well. They were in their late twenties and early thirties and were from a very different part of the country and a different culture. We had many interesting discussions as I got to know them and their way of life. In fact, their presence caused a big change in my menu—they liked everything spicy while I like bland food. They took turns cooking, but Mort seemed to be the meal specialist. One of the jobs he had in New Orleans was as a cook. Mort was also a magician. Every now and then he'd bring out some magic equipment and demonstrate this fascinating skill!

After the group settled in and we had a routine, they talked about their experiences in the hurricane in depth to me and another friend.

"At first I didn't have a clue a hurricane was coming," Ronnie Bruce said, "but when I heard about it, I decided to stay in my apartment. My building is two hundred years old and built like a fortress with huge brick walls and heavy cypress beams. It's probably the most secure place in the French Quarter. But then, my friend Lynn came looking for me. She was driving her friend's van out of the city and wanted me to go along. It took me five minutes to pack. We went to her place. Nine hours later she was still packing stuff in the car. Not just clothes but pictures, lots of stuff—probably a good thing. I passed the time doing Google earth on the computer and hanging out with her cat. We finally started out of the city on the causeway when we heard on the radio that the levy broke.

"I figured we'd go to Birmingham, Alabama, but half way through Mississippi I got a call from a friend, Nick, who said his eighty-year-old grandmother has a big house in Laurel, Mississippi, and we should all meet there. We were nearby so we changed plans. The place was huge and had a bomb shelter built during the Cuban missile crisis.

Six other ladies—friends of Nick's grandmother from the Gulf coast—were taking refuge at her house. One was blind, another one deaf, another was a psychic. I finally figured out Nick wasn't going to show up, but he wanted me to help out his grandmother. Slick Nick. So I cut down dangerous branches and stocked up on water. We heard that Katrina had hit New Orleans. Just before we headed to the bomb shelter, another lady who rents out trailer homes arrived with four Mexican families who needed shelter. At that point there was standing room only in the bomb shelter.

"Then the storm hit. Water started coming in. I was sure we were all going to drown, but it never got above my knees. We were all standing up anyway. When the storm passed, we went out to survey the damage. The house was fine, but the old sixty-foot-tall pines on the property were down with their roots pulled up. Twenty trees were on the driveway between the house and the highway. Two guys walked five miles to borrow a chainsaw. We finally got the trees cleared out with tractors, then we left for Memphis to try to meet up with some other friends at a hotel. We arrived and saw the news on TV for the first time. Not good. We started trying to get in touch with everyone we knew."

"Meanwhile, back in New Orleans, the four of us were watching the water seep into our first floor apartment," said Mort. "We moved our stuff up as high as we could onto shelves, then we reviewed our options." Tracy and Nathan explained that their place was about three blocks from the French Quarter, but "we didn't feel safe in that decrepit building so we grabbed what we could and went over to Kristina and Mort's apartment. We figured we'd spend the night. A few hours, the storm would pass, and we'd go home. But the water kept rising. We woke up with two inches of water on the floor."

"We were in the middle of it," said Kristina, "but we didn't really know what was going on. It was noisy, confusing and terrifying. Boats came by. We could hear helicopters overhead constantly. The next day the people from the second floor got airlifted out by helicopter because the guy was diabetic. They left us food, water and a phone and said to use their apartment."

"We moved upstairs. The water in our apartment rose to two feet," said Mort. "There was no electricity or water pressure."

"We had opportunities to leave," said Kristina, "but we couldn't because both Tracy and I had pets. I had a cat and dog and she had two kittens and a chinchilla. The boats wouldn't take us with the animals, so we had to stay until we could make arrangements for them to be picked up by the Humane Society. As it turned out, we left before they were rescued. We had to leave them with food and water and trust they'd be okay."

"We also had no idea of where we'd go once we did get out," added Mort.

"We were running out of food by then," said Nathan. "The police let us loot a gas station. I loaded up a floating Rubbermaid tote with peanuts and beef jerky. Normally I wouldn't do such a thing, but this was survival. I put plastic bags on my legs to wade through the water. It stank and was black with natural gas bubbles. The water's surface had a rainbow sheen."

"I was doing my best to keep myself supplied with protein and water and prenatal vitamins," Kristina added, "as well as trying to keep calm for my baby. I'm from Louisiana and I was wondering how my mother and grandmother were—they live just northwest of New Orleans."

Everyone went silent for a few moments. I could tell they were reliving those awful days of uncertainty. Kristina pulled a Kleenex out of the large purse that had accompanied her through it all, and then continued. "Communication was at a standstill for several days until the phones started working again. The relatives of the people who got out were calling to locate them. I took charge of the phone and passed on contact numbers for my neighbors. But we couldn't call out—only receive calls. I got one of the callers to contact my grandmother and Tracy's mom to let them know where we were and that we couldn't call out. We had to rely on this weird roundabout call chain. Somehow we managed to get the number to Ronnie Bruce and his friend Lynn who were looking for us.

"Once we made contact with them," said Kristina, "we started making plans. But it was a long process. Plans changed every hour. We were totally helpless. That was really scary—not being able to control anything or know if anyone was going to make that major effort for you. Now we know who our real friends are."

"The day we left," said Tracy, "we had to go out the back because the front door was locked, then wade through water to get onto the porch. We managed to flag down a fish and wildlife boat that had a camera crew with them. They wanted to take us to the convention center. That sounded like the ninth circle of hell. We told them we had people coming to the airport to meet us, so they took us by boat to a dry area in Carrollton uptown."

"By this time Ronnie Bruce had contacted Aileen and said we could stay with his grandmother in Minnesota. 'Sure,' we decided. 'Why not?'" said Kristina. "Various friends were arranging to get us to St. Louis then to Minnesota. But first we had to take a bus to Baton Rouge. It was terribly complicated, but we did it."

"When we started out, Nathan and I didn't have shoes or shirts. I did have a hat and my computer hard drive with me. We got clothes out of a pile of donations," said Mort. "There were so many others in worse shape around us—elderly folks, sick people, people who were upset. One man had a broken hip."

"At the same time we were following how our animal rescue was going," said Kristina. "My dog went to my grandmother's. We managed to stop and see her and my mom on our way out."

"My pets went to my mom in Oregon," said Tracy.

"My cat Kate is still unaccounted for, but I know she was picked up. I just need to track her whereabouts," said Kristina. "Considering everything, people really made a great effort and were very caring and careful with the animals."

They had lived through so much in such a short time. Their lives had been completely changed. It was quite a story and a lot of trauma. I was glad to be able to help out these young people. I especially liked our discussions. Conversations about ideas are not something I have with my kids. As I said to Heidi once, "Just wait till you get old. Most of the conversations one has are about nothing." Ronnie Bruce, especially, was great to talk to. We had amazing discussions and really explored topics. "You're opening up my brain," I told him. Our discussions made me feel vital and young.

I also had an interesting conversation with Nathan.

"I'm not too sure what life means," he said to me one day. "How do you get started? All I did in New Orleans was drift."

"I'll let you know what I know. I've lived almost a hundred years," I said. "The only thing I can tell you, Nathan, is that the value you put on yourself is the value other people see in you and understand. If you don't value yourself, no one is going to value you." That's all I told him. I don't know what he did with that answer.

After a month or so at the house, Tracy and Nathan moved to Minneapolis where there's a little more action and better chances of work. Kristina and Mort got the help and benefits they needed to rent an apartment not too far from me. They were joined by Kate, the cat, who had ended up in California and was flown to Minnesota. Their daughter Jade was born in early November—a Minnesota baby! Mort enrolled in a two-year computer graphics course at a technical school. Kristina found part time work and daycare for Jade. Ronnie Bruce stayed at my house and also spent time at his dad's place a few blocks away. He worked at a glass blower studio and studied Chinese.

The grandmother-grandson connection is very special. I felt a deep bond with Ronnie Bruce even though we weren't together that much. Mort told me once, "All the years I've known him, he'd say 'My grandmother did this, my grandmother says that.' He'd always bring up something about his grandmother."

Yet, I could sense Ronnie Bruce was getting restless. He told me his apartment in the French Quarter was still intact. I suppose he's thinking about New Orleans. He's living with Ron now and seldom comes over. Last fall he helped out in the yard and this spring he cleaned the leaves out by the north side of the garage.

One day he called to say he was coming over. "Grandma, I don't want to do this any more," he announced.

"That's interesting."

"I just don't want to live here. I don't like Minnesota. I'm thinking of going back to New Orleans."

"No chains. You're a free person," I told him. A few days later he had collected the things he had bought—some sturdy boots, a book or two, clothes, a laptop, and took off for New Orleans. He left behind his heavy winter jacket that we got him at the Goodwill. A week or so later Ron's assistant sent him an email. Ronnie Bruce answered that he had found a job and he was fine.

I was sad because I knew I'd miss him and I worried about him like any grandmother. But I felt really bad for Ron. He enjoyed having Ronnie Bruce live with him. Ron's speech actually improved because he had someone to talk to who meant a lot to him.

I asked Mort once, "You've known Ronnie Bruce for twelve years. What gives?"

"I don't know," he answered. "We'd be friends and do stuff together, then he'd disappear for a while and just as suddenly show up again."

It was two years before the borrowed bed and refrigerator were returned to their owners. Nathan sent a check and note thanking me for their stay at the house. That was the last any of us heard from Nathan and Tracy. Kristina moved back to New Orleans with Jade just in time to escape a very cold, long winter. Mort stayed on in Minneapolis.

Both Ron and I miss the connection to Ronnie Bruce. Maybe he was like Moses bringing his friends up here and leading them to new lives. I'm glad in my heart that I answered the distress call from my grandson.

✥ 33 ✥

My Variegated Life

I call it my "variegated life" as if it were a variety of plant—multicolored, dappled, spotted, and flecked. But that's me. My life has had highs, lows, and middles. Good times—lots of them—and bad times. Exhilarating events and happenings that shook me up. Moments when I knew my purpose and felt in harmony with everything and times of deep confusion. I've worked mainly as a nurse, but I also got certified as an ad litem court-appointed representative on behalf of children. I've tried my hand at real estate. Whatever I did, I was always energetic and very social. I enjoyed life when I was young and attractive. I enjoy life now when I'm finely aged and what they call "feisty."

Talking about age—I did my jump in June and then spent Christmas in Illinois with Heidi's family. Rachel's school held a Grandparents' Day and they showed my skydive video to the school kids. I notice that people look at me in one of three ways: As a fairly well-preserved specimen, as possibly a precious antique, or as someone who defies man, beast, and nature. I'm never too sure which concept people are working from when they are dealing with me.

Rachel had told me, "Many of the kids don't believe me." On the way home she said, "We showed them, didn't we?"

The 2004 St. Paul Winter Carnival featured an Ice Palace downtown. I decided to go. The ice palace is not built every year. With the changing climate, some years there's little or no snow and the ice sculptures melt! But someone must have prayed extra hard for a good freeze because that year the temperatures stayed well below zero. Despite the cold I didn't wear a hat. My blond wig kept my head plenty warm. I have a collection of wigs I used over the years so I would always look put together even after an all-night nursing shift.

A big part of the Winter Carnival tradition is the red-caped and masked Vulcan Krewe. The carnival ends when the Vulcans defeat King Boreas, King of the Winds, so that summer can return. A youngish Vulcan with black grease paint on his face came up to me.

"Having a hot time?" he asked with a grin.

"Not yet," I said. "What can you do about that?" Vulcans used to be notorious for inflicting sooty kisses on squealing women, but now they only give grease paint smudges to those who want them. We joked some more and posed for a photo. I enjoyed being regarded not as a well-preserved precious antique, but as just another fun-loving citizen of the frozen north.

I try not to let this aging thing get to me. It's attitude, you know. One of my attitudes is that I've gotta get it all done today! There may not be a tomorrow at my age.

It still shocks me to suddenly see myself as others see me, more so when it has to do with being vulnerable. I was in the grocery store pushing my cart and picking up what I needed when two nicely dressed older teens came up to me.

"Are you a grandmother?" they asked me.

I thought it was a strange question, but then they said, "We'd like to do some baking and don't know what to buy. Do you have a recommendation? We want to make chocolate chip cookies."

I had my purse in the cart in front of me and I kept holding on to the cart. But when I turned to the shelves to point out what they needed to buy, one of them snatched my purse and they took off.

I was so mad. I went to the store manager but the two were long gone. Between my anger at being victimized and all the work it took to replace my documents, I was a bit churned up. I had to really work at letting go and smoothing myself.

Of course, there are some distinct advantages to age and I know how to work them. I have a darling neighbor across the street. Marie is about fifty. I pick them young. On a sunny, late spring day she came over to help me rake the winter's salt and sand out of my yard along the street. She brought over a nice tall margarita. "You just sit down and have this margarita," she told me. "I'm going to clean the grass up." So I sat on the steps sipping my margarita and having a cigarette while she worked. She didn't have anything to do the next day so she offered to come over to help me cook too. I have great friends. I really do.

I'm also fortunate to still have my longtime neighbor Tina next door. She had her hair tinted for Easter. She lives alone even though she has macular degeneration and is blind. Her daughter helps her. Tina loves to go out for lunch. She was one hundred in September, but looks seventy. When I complain about being tired, she says, "Oh, I could do more than that at your age." When she could still see, she used to walk up to three miles most days. When I can't remember a date, I ask Tina. I'm eight years younger than she is. I sure can't say that very often.

I wonder every now and then why some people leave this earth when they are so desperately needed while others like Tina and me hang around.

I worked on an Alzheimer's ward at a nursing home for awhile. Some of the residents were clear about certain things and could manage themselves, and come and go, but others would wander off. I would go get Susan for dinner and knock on her door.

"Come in."

"Susan, it's time to eat now."

"I don't want to go down alone. Will you walk with me?"

She'd come over to me. Passing an urn sitting by the door, she'd say, "George, I'm going out to eat now. You can't yell at me about my cooking any more."

At least she was eating well and enjoying a respite from years of cooking for unappreciative George.

A strange thing about my variegated life is that I have claustrophobia like you wouldn't believe. I've always had it and still do. I'm not afraid to step out of a plane into thin air, but I think I could never go into a space shuttle. I can't watch a door close. If I do, it catches my throat. I don't think I'll ever get over that.

In high school I had to put the dumbbells away after gym class. I was in the closet and somebody went by and closed the door and it locked. There I was in a two-by-four space without an air vent. It totally frightened me. I began shouting, "Help, help, I'm dying!" Even now I never shut my bedroom door.

The problem is that I start hyperventilating. To control that, I breathe into a paper bag. Breathing carbon dioxide controls my hyperventilation for some reason.

On my trip home from Illinois to the Twin Cities I flew in a little plane. That provoked claustrophobia to an uncomfortable extent. I did get into that bitsy plane, though. I thought to myself, Isn't this amusing. I fit fine—I'm small but the other passengers and the stewardess have to move around with bent necks. To manage my claustrophobia, I try to focus on the funny side and see humor in order to distract myself. I can jump out of planes easy. Just don't seal me up in one.

Heidi and her kids came to St. Paul for a visit. Cleaning the house for days before they arrived nearly killed me. We went to the Mall of

America. She bought the kids fifty dollars' worth of ride tickets. Imagine—fifty dollars just to have kids go up and down and around. I told Heidi I was getting pretty tired even though I had been using an electric cart. She left me to get the kids. I thought I should go outside and get some air as I was also starting to feel claustrophobic. I walked over to the door, but I felt pretty weak so I headed back to my cart. When I got there I could barely move. An employee came over and asked me, "Are you okay?"

"I don't feel well," I said, "and I'm having trouble breathing." He called the paramedics. With them was a young guy being trained as a new paramedic.

"I can't find a pulse," he kept saying.

Finally I spoke up. "Look, kid, I'm not dead, okay? I'm sure I have a pulse." One of the more experienced paramedics took over.

Heidi finally came back with the kids. "What's the fuss, Mom? You didn't over-exert yourself. You were riding around on that cart the whole time."

To me my own death is no big deal, except that I want to clean things up otherwise people will be cussing me after I'm gone and I don't want to hear that.

I've seen many people die. There was the explosion at 3M that killed eleven people I knew who worked around me. As a private duty nurse, I attended dying patients. I remember one month eighteen people died. All that has given me a somewhat nonchalant attitude toward death.

For me it's just transformation, going from one state to another. I don't have a feeling of fear associated with death. If I jump out of airplanes, I'm obviously not going to sit around fearing death.

When people die, I feel sad. But I don't weep and mourn. My parents died, Joe died. My friends are dying. I don't cry. It's not in me. I think I was born like that. It is a tremendous pain to lose someone dear, but I remember the dead as they were.

I had the feeling that after my friend Julie's husband Stan died, she was just going through the motions of living for ten years. I think she was making an effort because that's how we Norwegian nurses from North Dakota are. You do what you have to do and you go on. But it seemed to me that she wasn't much interested in living. That basically shocked me. I wouldn't call it a negativism on her part. I'd maybe call it a retreat from life.

We had our nurses' bridge club and she was always a beautiful hostess. But with Stan's death, it was as if the essence had gone out of her life for her. It wasn't that she was morbid and it wasn't depressing to be with her. She would still laugh and tell stories. She'd get so disgusted at her son when he tried to get her to do things. "Sit up straight, Mom. Eat this healthy food I bought for you. Take this supplement." But it doesn't work by force of will.

It seems strange, though, because Julie had a very full life. She was always busy planning things and she did a tremendous amount of work. Julie was an independent person, too, but I really don't think anyone on the outside of married people's lives knows how they are intertwined. She didn't want to stay around anymore. I visited her several times when only her son was there with her and that's what I sensed. I brought her a crème brûlée on our last visit shortly before she died. I tried to be encouraging and positive. She wasn't having any of that. I don't remember if she even tasted the crème brûlée, but after a few moments she got up and left the kitchen table where we were sitting. She knew she was leaving here and she wasn't going to put up with anyone trying to tell her otherwise. That's how she was—basic with a sharp understanding of reality.

Not only did I lose a dear friend of many years, but the treasure box containing all that we shared and lived through is now closed. Tina, my dear neighbor of over fifty years, also died a few years later at age one hundred and one. Another treasure box closed. But I don't dwell on it. I'm living here in this present. That's where I keep my focus. Nobody else is going to do that for me!

My brother John Verner passed away in 1995 at seventy-two. John had a son Michael who was killed in a car accident. Michael's son was John's only grandchild. My sister Ruth was eighty-four when she died in 2003. I've outlived them both.

My relationship with Ruth was never close or smooth, although I did have contact with her kids and grandkids. Back in Towner growing up, Ruth was the one who taught Sunday school and was the exemplary Christian while I was the troublemaker. But then she married a man ten years older who was a dyed-in-the-wool atheist. Ruth became an atheist as well. Her husband Dale would go out of his way to make anti-Christian remarks. I did not like him and the feeling was mutual. My presence annoyed him so much that he usually retreated to his workshop in the basement when I appeared and stayed there until I left. He didn't believe in an afterlife so I'd tell him, "Well, Dale, say what you want, but I just have the feeling I'll still be around after I die."

I hope I'll still be able to laugh and joke when that time comes. My mother always said, "If you weep, you weep alone. If you laugh, the whole world laughs with you." So I've always laughed a lot. And I try to make others laugh along with me.

Recently we had a Neighborhood Council meeting that went on quite late. When I got dropped off after the meeting, the couple who gave me a ride spotted the red light on my garage and wanted to know the meaning of it. "It's my sideline," I said as I hopped out of the car. When the original bulb burned out, I picked up a new one at the hardware store but didn't check the color.

Speaking of outdoor lights, I've decided on a name for my veranda soiree, the late night get-together I hold by switching on my porch lights. I'm calling it "The Gathering." The other night I had six people out there at a Gathering. It was so much fun. Totally wild. Two were new to the group, but by the time everyone left, we were all buddies. One thing led to another. People were telling stories. Not gossiping, but telling stories about themselves, stories from life. They were all much younger and most were from the neighborhood. One fellow I've known a few years had gone someplace with his daughter and told her, "If Aileen's light is on, we'll stop." He was a former church member and had heard about my veranda parties. I thoroughly enjoy my reputation.

ᔥ 34 ᔥ

Family Matters

"**D**on't you dare die before I do."
These were my words to my daughter Heidi when she told me she had just been diagnosed with an aggressive form of breast cancer.

Heidi is forty-six. That's the age I was when I had her. When I first heard Heidi's diagnosis, it was as if someone punched me in the stomach. The news really hit me below the belt. I felt shattered inside. That is a crazy feeling for me.

It has been a struggle for me coping with Heidi's cancer. She's my very special daughter and we've been so close. We've taken trips together and I've visited her family in Illinois many times. I gave her Joe's accordion when he died and she plays it just like her dad.

My stepdaughter Joannie, who is very dear to me, had cancer a few years ago and recuperated. I want to remain hopeful and focus on Heidi's recovery. I don't shock easily, but Heidi's cancer was a real blow to me. Yet, I feel she will be fine.

Thanksgiving was special that year because Heidi was here with her family from Illinois. We had Thanksgiving at Mark and Charlotte's. It

216

was important that we could all be together after learning of Heidi's diagnosis. Even though we felt sad and worried, the occasion was upbeat and loving. I have always believed that God has his hand in all we do. Still, I never thought that I could be so mentally and physically down. The starch was really taken out of me. I've always been aware of problems and able to face them, but this put a new light on everything. All I could do was pray for help in the situation as it developed. I'm a firm believer in whatever will be, will be. I've never gone around trying to kid myself. It just doesn't work.

I told Heidi though, "You're lucky this happened now. There are so many new medical advances."

She had taken estrogen on her doctor's recommendation to help her through menopause. A doctor had wanted me to take it years ago, but I said absolutely not. That estrogen business is bad. The rate of cancer is up with all the hormones out there from birth control pills and hormone replacement therapy. I have always been a little nutty on the idea of those extra chemicals in the body. Of course, cigarette smoking supplies nasty chemicals. Heidi tried to get me to quit by putting up pictures of women smokers with terribly wrinkled faces. That got me to stop for a while but then I started again.

What bugs me is that Heidi's type of cancer is a silent type, practically undetectable. It is called Lobular Breast Cancer which doesn't have any calcifications so it doesn't show up on mammograms or ultrasounds. She had regular mammograms but nothing was detected. After she lost fifty pounds through Weight Watchers, she noticed that one breast looked perkier than the other. She thought it was due to working out, but checked with her doctor. The problem is that this type of cancer doesn't feel like the lump or bump that we are supposed to look for. Rather, it's a thickening under the skin, like a slab of liver underneath. By the time she saw the doctor, it was almost half the size of her D cup breast! She started chemo to shrink the tumor. After chemo, her doctors will see if they can operate.

My saving grace was the large, white artificial Christmas tree I brought up from my basement for Thanksgiving and set in a corner of the living room. My idea was to have Josh and Rachael, Heidi's two youngest children, decorate the tree to give them something to do. I don't have too many fun things for kids to do at my house. But we were too busy, and the tree stood in the corner all alone and bare. Then Heidi and her family left. I looked at the tree. It needed help. I needed help. I started decorating the tree myself. It was hands-on therapy. I sensed it would be self-healing to decorate it. I brought up all the ornament boxes from the basement. It was fun to hang my golf ornaments on the bottom, but they were heavy and the tree fell over backwards. I had to call my neighbor to anchor the tree. I took my time. I haven't had the big tree upstairs for six years. I'm usually away for Christmas and just put up a small tree. It took me about three days, but finally it was decorated and it was beautiful. It made my soul sing.

We all live each and every day with sad things happening. I feel that God must have a plan for me because he gave me improved eyesight and good health. Christmas 2006 with my daughter Heidi and her family had an extra-special meaning. It's amazing how difficult situations can arise when least expected and yet blossom and bring joy like a beautiful sunrise.

We had an early Christmas celebration at my house with Mark and his family and Ron. Then I went to Illinois for Christmas at Heidi's. We put a turkey in the oven so it would be ready when we came home from the 5:00 P.M. Candlelight Service on Christmas Eve. It was a beautiful service.

Heidi outdid herself decorating the house and the table setting was gorgeous. The Internet and Heidi were made for each other. On EBay she got a set of plates, cups and saucers, goblets, the works, all rimmed in gold for eighty dollars

Heidi's oldest daughter Jessica and her boyfriend were there that evening. Jessica's a glamour girl. She's in college working toward a marketing career. We ate first and then opened presents. The kids, though, were so excited about their presents that they couldn't finish eating. Heidi's family is full of love. It was such a joy to be with them.

On Christmas Day, Heidi's hair was hurting her because it was coming out in clumps, so she asked her husband Greg to shave it all off. He did it in the kitchen as I watched. It was so hard for me to watch my daughter go through that. She got sick right after he finished. My heart just sank! But Heidi is a survivor. She put on a wig and nothing more was said.

Rachael and Josh, Heidi's two young children, needed a lot of special nurturing because of their mother's sickness. So I told them more Oscar the Rabbit stories. Both kids crawled in bed with me as I related how he got shoved out of his home because developers took down all the trees to build houses. Oscar then decided to move over by the Lutheran Church. But, I told the kids, he still comes to my house every day. Oscar talks to me and tells me all his troubles. And then he listens when I tell him my troubles. He hops around my yard, and I put out extra food for him by the corner of my garage because he likes to eat there. It was kids on both sides of me and Oscar the Rabbit stories every night of my visit. Then it was time to fly back home where I would have a long bath and my own bed.

As I got off the plane, a gal in front of me asked if I needed help with my bags. "No," I said, "I just have this one suitcase on wheels, but can you tell me where the baggage claim is?" Mark was picking me up and I was supposed to meet him there.

"Sure," she said. "I can take you. I've got an hour before my next flight."

It turned out she'd been interviewed on David Letterman's show. "I'm a singer, songwriter, and I have my own band," she said.

"Three cheers for you!" I told her about skydiving and being on TV. We chatted and promised to keep in touch. We got the baggage and she called Mark to let him know where I was.

"You have a pretty sharp mother," she told him when he found us.

"I know," he said.

It was a good thing I had taken Heidi's dog out for walks twice a day because it seemed we walked miles before coming to the car.

"Oh, you can do it, Mom," said Mark. I certainly don't have to worry about being coddled by my family because I'm not.

Mark dropped me off at home and I took a relaxing hot bath for an hour and a half in my Jacuzzi. I thought, "Well, God, I'm ready to die happy."

Maybe I should have, because immediately another difficult situation appeared in my life. I pay Ron's cell phone bill. It usually runs about sixty dollars a month. Ron got a cell phone long before anyone else in the family. He realized a cell phone would be a big help to his communication, especially with an earpiece. He looks like he's wired to take off, but it works well for him. He programs the phone and he's just a phone call away from help. That's why it's so important to keep up the cell phone payments. But his bill was over six hundred dollars. I discovered he had been "treating" others to phone equipment and talking time.

Other bills followed. It turned out he was paying on six credit cards. I was shocked and very fearful that this was just the tip of the iceberg. I was afraid he was being exploited again and that he might lose his apartment. My ultimate fear is that he will be stuck in an institution.

I tried to sort through Ron's finances, assure his safety and respond to his future needs. What ensued was a bizarre situation that brought us into court and generated a court order stating that I could not have contact with Ron. That was a blow to me. I had taken care of him for nearly sixty years and now I was supposed to just drop him and the relationship. Who would get him to the doctor? Who would make sure his PCAs were doing their job? No one understands all his needs like I do, and no one else knows where to go in the social service system to deal with problems that come up.

I feel deeply protective of Ron. I felt like I was abandoning a baby and that part of this ordeal affected me the most. I'm used to resolving problems, yet suddenly my hands were tied. This was a crushing experience. I really wished I were either senile or dead!

Truthfully, those months of my life were very rough. Between my concerns for Heidi and having to figure out what was going on with Ron, I felt I was on the torturer's rack. I struggled to keep calm and to trust, but I'd have terrible nightmares about Ron and his safety. I recognized that it was necessary to set up a new permanent arrangement for him. I figured I probably wasn't going to live forever, but the whole process was very hard.

In the middle of it all, Ron had an accident with his scooter. He was going to the shopping mall near his house in the company of his aide when the wheel of his scooter hit a speed bump wrong and it tipped over. His PCA called the ambulance and Ron was in the hospital for several days then released to a county nursing home. Someone decided he needed twenty-four-hour care and started procedures to institutionalize him. What a trauma for us all, especially for Ron who likes his independent lifestyle.

I tried to calm my anxiety by recalling moments from the past like the time when Ron was about ten and had accompanied me to a luncheon with my friends. We were busy talking and passing maraschino cherries from our cocktails to Ron. Suddenly we noticed he was giggling and slipping down in his chair. He had gotten tipsy from the cherries!

When we'd go places and he was still able to walk, he would stand outside the door and wait for everyone to go in. Then he'd take my arm and we'd walk in together. Ron and I have had this special relationship for over sixty years. When I couldn't get around because of my back problem, he came over on his scooter from his apartment nearby to check on me.

I again questioned everything I had tried to do with Ron. I wondered about the kindness of putting a disabled child in with other children. I did have qualms about mainstreaming him. Had I pushed him too hard? But how can one gauge this? Was mainstreaming the best for Ron as a child—or did I do it mainly for my own gratification? Parents do a lot of things with kids for their own gratification. I acknowledge that I did. Again I wished I had resisted his pleas for that second surgery when Ron was a teen. Parents with disabled young adults have an especially hard time at that stage. Young people have a lot of frustrations that their parents can't cope with. I'll never forget the time Ron was coming down the stairs at home and fell. "You know, I can walk," he told me, sitting at the bottom of the steps. "I'm cured. I can walk," he kept repeating. How could I squash his spirit and say, "That's impossible," and that he'd never walk on his own? I never hammered in reality, even for myself! Ron tells me that in his dreams, he walks perfectly and even runs.

Even though I've had plenty of practice believing that things will turn out, it was hard to face letting go of sixty-plus years of constant caring for Ron. All these questions haunted me. Will he be all right? Who will make sure that his medical necessities are taken care of? Will he have people around him who will go the extra mile for him? The agency the court had appointed to manage his finances had already botched things up. If I hadn't checked to see if his rent had been paid, he would have lost his apartment and his housing assistance. No wonder I couldn't sleep well at night!

Several months before this whole situation came up, Ron and I both participated in a bike-a-thon fundraiser at the Xcel Center. I rode a stationary bike for four miles. Ron rode his electric scooter ten laps. I had sponsors for $150. The event raised a lot of money and we both got special tee-shirts.

Thinking back to the great efforts of a small group of people with disabled children and their families, I take pride in what we did. We really were able to promote acceptance of the disabled members of our community. Great strides have been made. People now have adaptive appliances, motorized scooters, barrier-free buildings and walkways. Local, state, and national governments are more aware and try to meet the needs of the disabled. The great fault is that there are few specific laws to protect people who don't need to be institutionalized and can live on their own. It often happens that they are victimized by the very people who are supposed to care for them.

My aim was to build a system to protect Ron from predators. Not only do I want to help Ron, who is considered a vulnerable adult, I'd like to help all people who need to be protected. I want to make the public aware of the dangers. We frequently hear about people who have been exploited by their caregivers or those in charge of their finances. This is an important cause for me and I will persevere in doing what I have done all along on this issue. I'm now ninety-three so I really have to work hard. Logic says I don't have too many years left.

I felt I was up one tree and down two others for awhile. Ron's rejection of me really hurt, but I took a long hard look at the whole picture. I realized I was mainly feeling sorry for myself and that was skewing everything else. I decided to wish Ron well. I had brought him up to think he could be his own person and be independent, and here he was, doing just that! Despite the ups and downs and what seemed like total disasters right and left, things eventually worked out. Heidi went through treatment and the necessary surgeries and survived. The court order was rescinded and Ron and I reconnected. His situation is much more stable. My son Mark, an extremely reliable and responsible person, offered to take over. I feel relieved now that Mark is Ron's guardian and the appropriate arrangements are in place for his care so that Ron is protected from further exploitation.

In retrospect, this should have been done before problems arose. Ron has deep respect for his half-brother Mark. The two of them have always been good friends. Now they work as a team, and Ron says, "Mark and I decided." He moved to a two-bedroom apartment in an independent living complex. Ron also has a devoted assistant, Lisa, who lives nearby and gives him the extra care and attention he needs. Ron's big dream is to be free of government aid, but until he strikes it rich in the stock market, this is the best he can do!

ಹ.35 ಆ

Come Fly with Me

One of my friends decided I should be a candidate for the 2008 St. Paul Winter Carnival Senior Royalty. I went to a couple of meetings and had to give a talk about myself. That's never a strain. I enjoyed it and had everyone laughing. The Senior Royal Court is made up of three men and three women who participate in Winter Carnival activities and appear at community events all year round. It would have been fun. I suspect I might have been selected for one of the titles because the organizers were very upset when I called them from the hospital after a fall and said I couldn't make it to the coronation. They told me to come in a wheelchair. But I had to decline. So much for being royalty!

"Come Fly with Me" was one of the titles I thought of for my book. I wanted to write the story of my life to fan the sparks of adventure in others. I believe we have this great opportunity—a life—and we should make the most of it with what we each have. Responding to life's challenges with a sense of adventure helps the spirit soar.

How to keep flying at any age? It's the mind! Tending the mind and keeping it constructive, even when it's hard, is the key.

225

I have been in excellent health all my life. But as I've, shall we say, matured, parts have worn out. That puts a stamp on my days. I'd love to be out golfing, out in the garden, or traveling around, but that's not to be. I find myself with limited energy and mobility. I didn't expect this, but who does? Even the brain checks out. As my friend Julie explained to me, "The parts of the brain that I used to count on to do things just aren't there anymore."

What's the point of this phase of my life? Well, I look at it this way. I've taken care of so many people for so many years that now I "get to" receive some taking care of—whether I want it or not. And there's always something to learn—whether I like what I'm learning or not.

What really bothers me now is not getting out into the garden regularly. My irises have gone to pot. Usually I dig them up every two years and reset the rhizomes, but I haven't been able to do that this year. I guess I'm learning about limits. I'm not exactly enjoying the lesson. I never allowed myself to believe in limitations. But now, knowing my limits actually helps me.

I have been fortunate all my life to have the energy to deal with the bumps in the road that we all have. Still, it was an unpleasant surprise to find out, at age ninety-four, that there was a big medical bump in the road.

When I ended up in the emergency room, they dragged out every test in the book. As I told the doctor puzzling over me, "That book you're looking through certainly is big. How many more tests are you going to find to give me?" The ER doctor was part Finnish. He had a sense of humor and talked to me like a real person. He said, "If I owned a car that was ninety-four years old, I'd expect a few things to go wrong with it. On some old cars the fenders fall off, some have motor trouble. Some cost more to repair than they are worth. That applies to people as well."

GETTING A JUMP ON LIFE

Being disabled is new to me. I call the condition resulting from my medical problems "being disabled" because it teaches me about what Ron and others have to face every day. It has bothered me terribly. But I put up with it. Besides, it seems as if I don't have a choice in the matter.

My stepdaughter, Joanniebell, has been a great help to me. I remember when we both worked at Miller Hospital before I had Mark. She was the nutritionist. I told everyone that we were sisters! She and I have grown a lot closer these last few months, although I'm sure I try her patience. "Don't mind me," I tell her. "I now belong to the moan and groan sorority." Imagine me after my hospital stay having to sit still in my house and entertain the nurses and aides who've been assigned to check up on me.

That reminds me of a story. One day, when I was still working at Miller Hospital and looking a lot more glamorous than I do now, I ran into a man and his wife in the supermarket. He greeted me in a warm, friendly way and gave me a big hug. Then he introduced his wife. All the while I'm wondering who in the world is this man and how do I know him. He could tell I didn't recognize him. Finally he said, "Don't you remember me from the hospital? I was your patient."

"Yes, but I don't recall your name," I fudged.

When he told me his name, I responded, "Oh, of course. I just didn't recognize you with your clothes on."

I've been a person who seldom looks back. Today is today. Yesterday is gone. Tomorrow isn't here yet. I don't look back on the "good ol' days"—even to the good days of being well. My theory is that I know it's bad, but it could be worse! Be strong, I say. Keep the faith!

I'm realistic and I know at some moment my time here will end and I'll be off on another adventure.

∗   ∗   ∗

Aileen's stay with us came to an end December 8, 2008. She thought she would be around longer—possibly to one hundred instead of the ninety-four and a half years that she lived. But her departure was marked by the same spirit with which she lived her life. Aileen had been having stomach pains for several months. Despite trips to the hospital, nothing was diagnosed until November when a fast-growing blockage was discovered. Medical solutions were tried but they failed. The doctors had given her six months to live, then they reduced that to two days. Aileen went home on a Friday under hospice care. Heidi had come by herself from Illinois.

That Saturday night, Aileen had her last party at her home of over fifty years. Her granddaughter Dianne painted Aileen's nails and she had her hair fixed. The word went out to family, friends, and neighbors who all crowded into Aileen's house to say their good-byes, toast to her, wish her well on her next journey, meet each other, and tell stories. Aileen was weak but witty, sad to be leaving but peaceful about her departure.

Sunday she rested from the party. Her pastor stopped by to see her, pray with the family and give them communion. On Monday evening, after Ron had visited and with her family around her, Aileen left on a new adventure.

The night she died, her granddaughter Rachael, Heidi's daughter, had a dream. Rachael and Josh were at home in Illinois. As she tells it, "The same night I heard that Grandma died, I had a dream that she was rubbing my back and saying, 'Don't be sad. Don't cry.' It really felt like Grandma was there rubbing my back. That made me feel good. Then she told me some Oscar the Rabbit stories."

Ron believes his mother is watching over him. Lisa spent time at Ron's place after Aileen died. The night she passed away, Lisa went into Ron's room to check on him at 2:00 A.M. and the smoke detector beeped. "That's Mom," Ron said. "She's protecting me."

The next evening Lisa had prepared supper and they were sitting down to eat when they heard footsteps outside the door. Lisa went to the door, but no one was there.

Lisa had purchased a terrier puppy for her daughter and kept it at Ron's for a few days. Every now and then the dog started to growl for no apparent reason. "We think he sensed Aileen's presence," she said.

"Mom's spirit is in this house," Ron says. "And she's with me every night in my dreams."

Aileen's funeral-memorial service was held a few weeks later. The night before the funeral, Charlotte, Mark's wife, dreamt that she was with Aileen in the women's room at church as if they were getting ready for a wedding. Aileen was dressed in pink. That's the color she chose for her ninetieth birthday skydive. In the dream Aileen asked her, "What's going on?"

"It's your funeral," Charlotte told her.

"Oh, I'm not dead. Let's go in there and show them I'm alive."

Aileen's actual funeral was a celebration focused on her life. Family members got together who hadn't seen each other in many years. Friends and family met and shared many stories about Aileen. Her pastor, the Rev. Charlie Brown, who had visited her often the last few months, recalled the highlights of her life.

Heidi decided to stay and have Christmas Eve at Aileen's house with the family. She set up the white Christmas tree and used her mom's decorations. It was just like Christmas at Aileen's except that Aileen wasn't there. Or was she? Greg got the gas fireplace going which was what Aileen always asked him to do. The gas fireplace had been on for a few hours. At one point Greg noticed that the flame had gone out. As he approached the fireplace, the flames spontaneously reignited. He turned to Jessica who remarked, "That's really weird. Do you think that's Grandma?" Greg responded, "I've sat by this fireplace for years and I've never known it to go out and ignite all by itself."

Later on that evening, from across that room, Greg noticed that flame was out again. He told Jessica to watch the fireplace as he approached it. As Greg drew near the fireplace, it spontaneously ignited with a large flame. Greg and Jessica stared at each other in stunned silence. Heidi saw it too and said, "It's Mom letting us know she's here with us! Mom and I agreed that, if possible, she would communicate with me by turning something on and off. The fireplace—how perfect!"

Mark and Heidi decided to sell Aileen's house as soon as they could move things out and clean it. It sold within three weeks of being put on the market. Mark, Charlotte and Joannie had all come to say good-bye to the house, now empty and thoroughly cleaned. In a few days the new owners would move in. Mark was upstairs alone. "I felt like I wanted to say a prayer as part of my good-bye," he said, "but I didn't know what to say. Then I looked down and saw a piece of paper on the floor. It was a clipping from a old newspaper with a prayer to Mary on it. As I said the prayer, I remembered that Mom promised she would always be with us. That was her last promise to us. I truly felt her presence."

Ron faces an additional health challenge. He has prostate cancer. But he says his mom helps him when he gets down. "She cheers me up. She says, 'Don't think about it. Just live one day at a time.' I remember the things she taught me like 'Never give up. Keep trying. Be positive.' That's what I do."

Aileen would have been ninety-five on June 27, 2009. That was the day Heidi planned to have Kerry McCauley from Skydive Twin Cities release some of Aileen's ashes while skydiving. However, bad weather forced postponement to the following week. Dianne, Joannie's daughter, quipped, "Well, I think Aileen didn't want to have the jump on her birthday because she never liked acknowledging her real age."

Mark was there along with Heidi and Greg and their kids Josh and Rachael. Patty, the talented woman who taught Aileen stained-glass making and created her parrot window, also came. Joannie, Dianne and her husband Tony and their twins Noah and Samuel along with Aileen's niece Helen, her husband Clint, and their children Holly and Teddy, all gathered at the airstrip in Wisconsin that serves as Skydive Twin Cities' headquarters. Tony designed the cake decoration of a blue sky with clouds and the words "One Last Jump for Aileen."

It was a busy day at the airstrip and while everyone was waiting for Aileen's turn, Kerry elaborated on the jump plan. After freefall and dancing for Aileen, he would set off the smoke canister on his ankle before releasing her ashes.

Then he added, "I've never said anything about this before, but there was a malfunction on Aileen's first jump. The guideline got tangled in the parachute. The usual procedure," Kerry explained, "is to cut the chute away and go with the reserve parachute. But I decided to try to work the line free. The experienced skydivers watching on the ground realized what was happening. I knew they wanted me to cut away, but I persisted and got the line free and the jump proceeded as normal. I didn't think it would be too good to have a malfunction on national TV," he said.

Aileen's last jump went according to plan. On a clear, sunny July 5th her friends and family watched the white puff of her ashes dissipate into the blue sky. Those who knew her are sure that Aileen's spirit is soaring and will continue to touch others through her words and the laughter she loves to provoke.

✍ Appendix ✌

Eulogy for Aileen Helen Fritsch
December 19, 2008
Delivered by Jacqueline Mosio

It's hard to believe that Aileen has left us. Who will make us laugh at the ups and downs of life? Who will entertain us with her exploits and adventures? Who will teach us about living life with verve, nerve and her special sense of humor? Remember her license plates? They say RETREAD.

She surprised us all with her skydiving, but it was totally in character. She challenged herself and inspired folks around the world. Then she decided to tell her life's story in a book. "When people read it," she said, "they'll say 'No wonder she wanted to jump out of plane.'"

I have had the great and treasured privilege of working with Aileen these last four years, interviewing her, taking notes, writing her story, and deepening a friendship I inherited from my mother.

Aileen was a friend of my mother's from nurses' training at St. Luke's Hospital and she became a close friend of the family. Aileen was fascinating to me. As a young girl I watched this slim, self-confident, energetic woman sweep into the house. She came with Ron holding her hand and smiling at her side. Aileen was a private duty nurse who worked at the homes of the wealthy. She had an aura of mystery and adventure about her. All of this was very intriguing to me. Aileen joked, teased, and told stories that kept us laughing.

She'd tell stories from her North Dakota childhood like when she decided to give her squalling fussy little brother to the gypsies, or when she put frogs in a teacher's desk, or the time she and a friend ate all the communion wafers in attempt to become holy.

Aileen graduated a year early from high school and attended the University of Minnesota with the idea she would be a doctor and a surgeon. But after the first year, her family could no longer afford the tuition—this was during the Depression—so she went into nursing.

She loved nursing and caring for others. It gave her many opportunities to get to know people—and gave her an endless supply of stories.

One day, when she was still working at Miller Hospital, she ran into a man and his wife in the supermarket. He greeted her warmly and gave her a big hug and introduced his wife. She had no idea who he was.

"Don't you remember me from the hospital? I was your patient."

"Yes, but I don't recall your name."

He told her his name. "Oh, of course," she said. "The problem is that I just didn't recognize you with your clothes on."

Every phase of Aileen's life had its stories and I'm sure you have your favorites.

Her first car was a tiny blue Crosley that the engineers at 3M where she worked as an industrial nurse would carry into the building as a joke.

Ron's bird Petey who dive-bombed the mashed potatoes in the crown roast just before Aileen was going to serve it to his teachers for dinner.

There was the trip to New York and Washington on the back of her son Mark's motorcycle.

The Tiffany-type lampshade she bought in Mexico and wore onto the plane as a hat because the airline official wasn't going to let her carry it onboard.

Aileen was a master of one-liners: "I didn't come under last year's Christmas tree, you know."

Aileen took life's challenges and life's fun seriously. She rode horseback, danced, golfed, knitted, partied, and traveled starting soon after she graduated from nurses' training. But once Ron was born, she pledged she would take care of him the rest of her life. She did that. She fulfilled her promise to him and to God.

She was a single mom raising Ron for several years before she met and married Joe, Mark and Heidi's father, and Joan's father. She continued working. She raised a family, cared for her aging parents, traveled to China, Syria and Europe as well as all over the U.S. She visited with her grandchildren, great and great-great grandchildren. We all remember how she opened her house to her grandson, Ronnie Bruce, and his four friends, refugees from Hurricane Katrina in New Orleans.

She was fond of saying, "It's a great life—if you don't weaken."

As I worked with Aileen, I wanted to know, "What makes her tick? What keeps her going?"

She talked about her firm sense of faith, her conviction that God would take care of things if she did her part and worked hard.

Underneath the banter and story-telling and adventuring was a woman who not only loved and cared for others but had a strong, steady relationship with God, who talked to him.

Her daughter Heidi said to her a few years ago, "Mom, I don't know—how do you figure you have a direct line to God? Nobody else beeps in. You've got it all settled."

Aileen answered, "Ever since I was young, I talked to God. I talked about the people I knew, what things happened. I thank him. It's like I lift a telephone receiver and talk direct. I pray for other people and hope God remembers them. I believe in a divine power. Yes I do."

Her neighbors will always remember that in the evenings, especially in the summertime, she'd put her special porch lights on. That was a signal to the neighbors to come on over with their own drinks and join her on the porch for conversation and companionship late into the night. I think Aileen knew how much her family and friends would miss her, so she decided to leave her book as a gift to us all.

Heidi and I asked her, during her last days, how she wanted to dedicate the book. She said, "To all the people I love."

Captain Ekstrom

*R*eminiscences as told by Capt. Ekstrom to his daughter Mrs. I.B. Cook, when he was ninety years old. (Reproduced from a family manuscript.)

I was born in Erbro, Sweden on January 20, 1845. I was the second youngest in a large family and the only living member at present.

My father Peter was wealthy, being interested in a line of freighters that visited the leading countries of the world at that time. When the boats would dock in the harbor, I would, in spite of the fact that I was a mere child, accompany him on his tour of inspection. While Father was transacting business, I would play on the decks and climb the riggings. It was at this time that I decided that as soon as I was old enough I would be a sailor.

At fifteen I graduated from high school and had the opportunity of entering the university, but my only desire was to sail the seas. The first year I spent on a Boys' Training Ship in Stockholm. At sixteen I had to return home to receive instructions for Confirmation. This was compulsory as the law of the land was that every child at the age of sixteen must be confirmed.

My parents pleaded with me to give up this notion of being a sailor but to no avail. I finally received permission and after obtaining my recommendations, I started for Gottenborg. The trip was by coach over rough roads. In this coach were two Jewish priests (sic) and a corpulent woman beside whom I sat. I arrived in Gottenborg late in the day, it was foggy and misty. I had an address to a boarding house for students. After wandering around for some time I asked a policeman for information, and he directed me to the house. I rapped on the door and a middle-aged woman appeared. I introduced myself and handed her a letter. After she had read the letter she was very cordial and invited me in.

I was very tired after my long ride. The next day I interviewed a Captain whose boat was ready to sail. After reading my recommendations he decided to accept me and ordered me to change my clothes and get to work. There was another lad who was so ill-behaved at home that his parents had sent him on this boat thinking it would tame him down a bit.

The name of the first vessel I sailed was Julia. All the sailors occupied the same cabin. The bunks were crude and built one over the other. There was very little space to move about. Before we left we were given our rations which had to last for a certain length of time. Also we received a tin plate, soup bowl, tin cup, fork and spoon. Our pocket knife had to be used as a substitute for a table knife.

Our breakfast was black coffee, mush and hard tack; dinner was pea soup and supper was pea soup, salt pork, hard tack and black coffee. Thus was our daily diet except when we anchored at some port, then we received fresh meat, vegetables, fruit, etc. The boat had no facilities for keeping perishable foods on long trips.

I experienced several ship wrecks. The first was in the North Sea. This was about Christmas time. For days a raging blizzard tossed the ship about, carried away the main mast and the forecastle. The boat was covered with ice and snow. The ropes which controlled the sails were also covered with ice. We took turns climbing the riggings and pounding the ice off the ropes. One sailor, an older man, was swept into the sea. When the storm subsided, the boat had drifted along the northern coast of Norway. A pilot and his twelve-year-old grandson came to our rescue. He was asked to pilot the boat to shore. We threw a rope to him and pulled him on board. The little lad took the pilot's boat back to shore.

The town was a fishermen's village called Cleveland. (*This name was difficult for me to read so I guessed at it. It may not be correct. I copied this from my mother's handwritten copy of this story.*) Here we were treated very kindly by the people. That night was Christmas Eve. We spent it drying our clothes and retiring early. Our beds were made by scattering hay on the floor. We were given blankets; we laid down and were glad to rest. As I lay there I thought of the Christmas Festival which was taking place at my home. The lad who hired out on this boat was glad to go home and behave himself, but I was determined to carry on.

The second ship wreck was off the Danish coast. As the tide went out we gathered our belongings and went ashore. We told the fisher folks they could have what they could salvage from the ship in exchange for food. This they gladly did saying, "It was the first time God had blessed them for two years."

I returned to Gottenborg and signed up with one of the largest, finest boats which would be ready to sail in about two or three days.

I wrote mother telling her about my plans. Mother telegraphed Gottenborg asking me to wait because she was coming to see me. Before she arrived our boat had started out. Mother chartered a steamer and followed for some distance in hopes she could encourage me to come home. We watched the steamer from our dock thinking that tourists were out on a pleasure trip, little realizing my mother was on board.

When I reached Australia a letter was waiting for me. The mail had gone over land. It required 128 days to make this voyage. Australia was a new country and alive with excitement over the finding of gold.

On one of our stops at Bombay there was another boat called the Red Jacket. They challenged four other vessels in a race to Liverpool. The captain of our boat wished to enter the race but the Insurance Company objected. The prize was $2500. The vessels left Bombay before our vessel did, however our captain decided to try to best the other vessels. It required 122 days to make the trip. We won the race reaching Liverpool 48 hours before one vessel and four days before the second vessel. Crowds of people gave us a great welcome.

I returned home after having spent 39 months sailing.

The next boat I went aboard was the Elanor. We had a mixed cargo from Liverpool to Archangel. The ice had been reported out but as we entered the White Sea, the current brought back the ice. This was in the month of May. Our vessel was caught in the ice jam and crushed. We left our vessel hanging on the ice and started on foot to reach land. This was about four or five o'clock P.M. We saw seven other vessels wrecked. We walked about one hundred miles and when we became tired, we would lie down on the ice to rest and then to go on again. Our food was pork and snow.

We traveled for two days and one night this way. We thought we saw land, started again the next day and finally did see land at four P.M. All we could see was sand and brush. The nearest town was Cola. As we were gazing for some sign of life, one of the boys saw some smoke in the distance.

We traveled on until we reached a village inhabited by Finlaps, very small people about five feet or less tall. Their huts were made of drift wood and covered with seaweed. The large room was about twelve by sixteen feet with a rock fireplace in one end. It was very neat. They lived on fish, reindeer and barley bread. The milk from the reindeer was given to the children. A father and son took the Captain to Cola for supplies. The Captain wired Archangel and learned that crews on other vessels had perished.

After this I attended school at Gottenborg and received my title as Captain but sailed as first mate. I was called home because of [economic] depression. I stayed home for one month and started out again. I left for Liverpool seeking work but the depression was general. Finally I left for New York. Here I found conditions worse as the Civil War was just over and commerce was at a standstill. My pal and I left for Chicago and from there we went to St. Paul. The farthest west the railroad had reached was St. Cloud.

I liked the country and purchased two quarters of land from Col. Matteson. I paid between $180 and $200 for a yoke of oxen. I broke twelve acres of land and I raised a good crop of wheat but had to haul it two miles to market. The price I received was 52 cents a bushel. Flour cost five dollars per hundred. I was able to haul only thirty bushels on account of the bad roads.

The grasshoppers destroyed the crops for the following three years and the fourth year a tornado destroyed everything. I finally sold the farm for $1,500 cash and $3,000 on time with interest at (*this looked like ten percent but it was very difficult for me to see*). The farm was finally known as the Weard Farm.

Mother and I were married in St. Paul on April 20, 1872. We lived on the farm for a couple of years then decided to move into town where I opened an Abstract and Real Estate Office. I was Sheriff of Meeker County and preferred to go alone to get my man and I never failed to bring him back.

After being Sheriff, I was Auditor and Collector for the following machine companies: Plano, John Deere and McCormick, at times having the eastern half of North Dakota as my territory. At this time my hearing began to fail and it was necessary for me to give up this type of work.

In 1898 I came to Towner and have been here ever since, but for my sight and hearing I am in perfect health.

There were many places of interest I visited while at sea. One [was] an island in the Mediterranean Sea off the Coast of France where the Count of Monte Cristo was held as prisoner. The Black Hole of India where so many British soldiers perished and a Church on the Spanish Coast of the Mediterranean where the Inquisition was practiced. In this church I saw the terrible means that were used in executing unfortunate victims. The stone steps were worn from people walking down to their awful death. In the chambers where they were sentenced were the huge chairs where the judges sat. When I saw the places of torture, it seemed the blood stains were still noticeable. I have seen the funeral biers on the shores of India. At one time I witnessed the execution of twelve Malay pirates by the Danish man of war. This put an end to piracy in this region and it was safe to travel between the peninsula and the East Indies.

Well, I believe that is all I can recall now. A few years ago I could have related the things as they happened, even the dates on which they occurred.

I have sailed around the world thirteen times and the only coast I haven't seen is the Pacific coast of the United States. This was not open to travel.

Obituary

Captain P. Ekstrom was born in Erbro / Orebro, Sweden, January 20, 1845. He came to the U.S. after the Civil War and located at Litchfield, Minnesota before the railroad reached there. He was one of the last pioneers of that section to pass away.

On April 20, 1872, he was married to Helen Sandow / Helena Sauvrow. There were six children, two passed away in infancy. The remaining members are: Karin, Mrs. C.H. Gumelius; Anna, Mrs. I.B. Cook; Jon Ekstrom; Mamie, Mrs. Fred Hermanson of Seattle, Washington. The others all live at Towner, North Dakota. There were eighteen grandchildren, one Edna Karin Ekstrom passed away at the age of two. The remaining grandchildren are: Arvid Gumelius, Helen Hattie, Lytle, LeRoy and Pat Cook; Robert and Esther Hermanson and Aileen, Ruth and Verner Ekstrom.

Captain Ekstrom passed away at his home April 29, 1938. Funeral services were held in the (sic) on May first with the Rev. Basil Dourthy of the Episcopal Church officiating. The following were present at his funeral: two daughters, his son, five grandsons, Arvid Gumelius, Verner Ekstrom, Lytle Cook from Hatton, North Dakota, LeRoy Cook from Hillsboro, North Dakota, and Irvin (Pat) Cook from Grand Forks, N.Dak., and a granddaughter, Hattie Cook, from Rugby, North Dakota.

His daughter, Mrs. Fred Hermanson and children and Helen Cook from Seattle, Washington, were unable to attend. Aileen and Ruth Ekstrom from St. Paul were also unable to attend.

Links and Contacts

Email: gettingajump@comcast.net

Publisher's web site: www.northstarpress.com

Video clips of Aileen's appearances on CBS TV *The Early Show*:

June 2004
http://www.cbsnews.com/stories/2004/06/29/earlyshow/living/main62
6609.shtml

June 2005
http://www.cbsnews.com/stories/2005/07/06/earlyshow/living/main70
6773.shtml

Look for more information about Aileen Fritsch on **Facebook** and on her web site **www.gettingajumponlife.com**.